A Christian Worldview
Essays From
A Reformed Perspective

A Christian Worldview
Essays From
A Reformed Perspective

EDITED BY

C. N. WILLBORN

Presbyterian Press
P.O. Box 770, Taylors, SC 29687

© 2008 by C. N. Willborn

Presbyterian Press

P.O. Box 770
Taylors, SC 29687
www.presbyterianbookshop.com

Printed in the United States of America

A Christian Worldview: Essays From A Reformed Perspective
edited by C. N. Willborn
p. cm.
Includes bibliographical references.
ISBN: 1-931639-12-4
1. Apologetics

Table of Contents

ACKNOWLEDGMENTS

The articles that make up the body of this volume were prepared for the annual Spring Theology Conference sponsored by Greenville Presbyterian Theological Seminary in Greenville, South Carolina. I wish to thank the gentlemen who prepared and delivered them before several hundred folk in attendance last March for allowing us to present them in published form. The centerpiece of the two evening sessions of the Conference is always an exposition of Holy Scripture and these sermons have been transcribed for us by Thomas Gormley of Audioposting, to whom we give our thanks. I also wish to thank Mrs. Caroline Q. Brown, Mr. Breno Macedo, Mr. Andy Wortman, Mr. Daniel Wilson, and Dr. Benjamin Shaw for their able attention to various editing, formatting, and design details that make this book more attractive and useful. I'd be terribly remiss if I didn't thank my able friend and help-meet Carol for all she does to see that I get projects like this finished—somewhat on time. Above all, I thank the One who is preeminent in all things, our covenant faithful God and pray that this book brings Him honor for He is "a great King above all gods" and "greatly to be praised." SDG!

Introduction

C. N. Willborn

David Wells has asserted and demonstrated (if it needed more demonstration than is easily apparent all around us), "Evangelicalism, now much absorbed by the arts and tricks of marketing, is simply not very serious anymore." The culture of the world has become the culture of the church in many ecclesiastical circles.

From another angle, I just heard a leading Christian observer state that younger evangelicals are not so concerned with issues like sanctity of life and sexual preferences—matters to which the Bible speaks quite loudly—but rather with environmental rights and the likes. Culture creeps in and the voice of God-breathed Scripture recedes.

Indulge me again—turn on the television or radio, log on to the web, and you can hear (and read) an awful lot about the spiritual and spirituality. Prominent journalists interview Hollywood dons, political aspirants, and international moguls, and often, if not always, ask them if they are "spiritual" or inquire as to their "spirituality." People everywhere speak of their "faith"—the object of which is seldom questioned.

In a day when popular Christianity isn't serious any more and culture has become revelation to many and faith is spoken of apart from the Triune God who alone can authenticate it, there is much need to speak seriously about serious matters in our world. This little book does just that. These essays were delivered at the annual Spring Theology Conference of Greenville Presbyterian Theological Seminary in 2007.

While the essays are of a more popular tenor, and are not highly technical or philosophical, they display a certain gravitas toward the issues of our day. Some of the topics will not surprise you. The near ubiquitous issues of informational technology and Islam are treated as most readers would expect. There is a biographical sketch of a dead Calvinist who influenced the whole topic of "World view"—no surprise.

But, we do treat you to a few topics that may—although they really shouldn't—strike you as peculiar. Here I have in mind the topics of Roman Catholicism and War. Christians today are so uncritical of "religion" and "spirituality" that they do little constructive thinking about anything that claims to be "Christian" or, even, that which talks a lot about "God." So, we tackled Romanism as a most important topic. At the same time, our nation is involved in its "war against terror" and military troops are serving us in combative stations abroad, some giving their lives for the cause of freedom. Pacifists question war in general; growing numbers question the "just war" claim. We provide a starting point for what we think is right thinking on the matter. As if these are not enough, we transcribed one of the evening sermons to remind us all that our world view is uniquely structured around the pivotal person in the history of fallen humanity, Jesus Christ. And, finally, I should mention there is an essay which should help many of us think more accurately about the world around us—taking every thought captive—from a particularly Reformed perspective; we begin the book with this foundational piece.

I am certainly aware that the topics covered in this volume are not exhaustive and, therefore, will not "fit the bill" of a textbook. However, it was our intention to provide timely and insightful discourse on some foundational matters of a Christian Worldview and some particularly interesting and current topics. We often read about "culture wars" and they certainly exist and enter into the world view discussion. But there is also what I call the "consciousness war." By that I mean that we often meander through life with a less than acute consciousness. It's not that we're unconscious, but we are dull, our sensitivities all too easily become blunted. We can lack acumen when thinking about all the political, social, and religious ideas that whirl around our heads and blow through our mental filters on a daily, even momentary basis. Thus, these essays are given to challenge our thinking and whittle away at those senses that may have grown thick or blunt and, in turn, heighten and hone the consciousness of our readers. Readers may not always agree with the position or assessment of a given author. Although I would hope these essays are persuasive, I hope just as much that they are as a grinding wheel to metal, which sharpens to greater usefulness. They are offered by Christian pastors and scholars as iron to sharpen iron.

As a culmination to the varied essays, the reader will find a transcribed and edited sermon on "The Exclusiveness of Christ." To the thinking Christian this won't seem odd at all, but all the more appropriate and satisfying. In his enduring treatment of *The Christian View of God and Man,* James Orr argued: "He who with his whole heart believes in Jesus as the Son of God is thereby committed to much else besides. He is committed to a view of God, to a view of man, to a view of sin, to a view of Redemption, to a view of human destiny, found only in Christianity." With this in mind and in agreement with Orr, the concluding chapter of our little book sets forth Jesus as the Exclusive One *in* Whom one believes and *by* Whom one may make sense of it all.

Chapter 1

The Reformed World View

K. Scott Oliphint[1]

INTRODUCTION—TERMS AND DEFINITIONS

Our topic is "The Reformed World View," on which we could spend hours, if not days, because of the diversity of definitions that swirls around each of these words—What do we mean when we say "Reformed" or "World" or "View"?

Such questions are important, even if perhaps somewhat pedantic, but we will forego any temptation toward a laborious *logomachia* and attempt to be more general in our initial foray into this topic. That said, a few clarifying points may help.

First, though the *idea* of a world view has been around since the beginning of time, it is fair to say, it seems to me, that the topic as a specific discipline with specific terminology came into its own, as one might expect, during the Enlightenment. Before entering into the reason for that, we should briefly note the relevance of this topic in the current context.

THE CURRENT CLIMATE

Second, we should initially acknowledge the effects that postmodernism has had on our understanding, generally, of the notion of

---

[1] Scott Oliphant PhD is Professor of Apologetics and Systematic Theology in the Westminster Theological Seminary, Philadelphia, Pennsylvania and an ordained minister in the Orthodox Presbyterian Church.

"world view." We should realize, however, that postmodernism seems to be on its last leg. I suspect that within a few years it will be all but dead.

This should teach us something that we in the church often have difficulty learning. Whenever we give undue weight to the latest philosophical or cultural fad, that part of our thought becomes obsolete when that fad dies. Too often Christians argue as if being relevant means tying ourselves to the current trend. Yet if history tells us anything, it tells us (1) that every philosophical and cultural trend comes on the scene and then dies and (2) the current philosophical and cultural trend is itself destined for death. This does not mean that we should ignore the trends, it only means that we should see them for what they are—fads. While no one is sure of the origin of the word 'fad,' I do like the way some have seen it as an acronym standing for 'for a day.' That's what philosophical trends are – it was that way in the beginning, is now, and ever shall be.

Having said that, how should we think of the relationship between world view and postmodernity? That would, of course, depend on what we mean by postmodernity. For the sake of simplicity, let's stick with Lyotard's notion of what he calls an "incredulity toward metanarratives." Just what he means by that has been a topic of furious debate, but we must start somewhere. The driving force behind postmodern thinking is that there can be no overarching system of thought, or world view that has hegemonic influence over every other. An incredulity toward metanarratives simply means that we don't believe anything that attempts to stake its claim on some kind of universality.

How then does the notion of postmodernism relate to a discussion of world view? According to one source, we may be at the end of the age of world view. Paul Marshall, Griffoen Sander, and Richard J. Mouw, in their discussion of the pluralism entailed in postmodernism, write the following: "Such stark pluralism can no longer be described as a *Streit der Weltanschauungen* [conflict of world views], for world views can conflict only if they compete as accounts of the same 'world.' In the extreme pluralism of...[postmodernity], there is no single 'world' – there are as many worlds as there are world views. It is possible...that we are now on the threshold of the end of the age of world views."[2]

There are a few problems with this analysis, not the least of which is allowing the current fads of the day to determine the existence or lack

---

[2]   This quote, and the material immediately following, are dependent on David K. Naugle, *Worldview: The History of a Concept* (Grand Rapids, Michigan\Cambridge, U.K.: William B. Eerdmans Publishing Company, 2002), 174ff.

thereof of a world view. For this analysis to be correct, world views would have to be strictly and purely subjective, which is questionable, especially from a Christian perspective.

Having said that, there is little question that, if postmodernity had its way, world views would be altogether non-existent. As a matter of fact, Jacques Derrida would have us believe that, in spite of our long tradition in the West of regarding things like world views as real and influential concepts, they are, in the end, nothing more than a part of our modernist illusion. Because of our Western 'logocentrism,' we have sought for something that transcends language to give it its meaning—a 'transcendental signified.' That transcendental signified has been purported to be the Absolute, the Idea, and a number of other things. Behind these notions, however, according to Derrida, is the 'metaphysics of presence,' which is his way of saying that we have assumed that there is something ultimate that is real. Derrida argues that we cannot access reality; there is no knowledge of a pre-linguistic, preconceptual Idea of Spirit. Thus, logocentrism, attempting to reflect reality through language, and the metaphysics of presence, are both wrong-headed.

What's a world view-ish person to do? There are a number of responses that could be given, but we'll mentions just three briefly. First of all, the reason that the heyday of postmodernism is over so quickly is because its theories were never able seriously to be entertained, in part due to the outrageous positions that were touted by Derrida, Rorty and others. These positions were not able to catch on because they were rarely ever argued, and when they were argued there was little of substance or clarity in the arguments themselves. Not only so, but to argue the position is, in effect, to deny its central tenet.

The second thing that must be said is that there are some, though perhaps only a few, who wish to see in much of postmodernism a kinship with the Christian faith. In a collection of essays in the book *Overcoming Onto-theology*, Merold Westphal attempts to make the point that what postmodernism was critiquing was *not* Christianity, but rather Hegelian and Marxian notions of history. Westphal's contention is that postmodernism is not concerned with *every* world view, but rather with any "story" that would seek to subsume everything else under it. Of course, whether or not postmodernity had its roots in a rejection of Christianity is not especially relevant. What *is* relevant is whether or not postmodernity is, in the main, hostile to the Christian faith.

Thirdly, we should note that in much of postmodernism there is thought to be an inextricable link, what we might call a *necessary* link between language and thought. This, of course, seems to be Derrida's position, with certain twists and nuances that have to do with his idea of *différance*. This was also the case in Gadamer's hermeneutics. The purpose of this, of course, is to demonstrate why it is that we can have no access to the horizon of existence, or to reality itself. This is, in one sense, full-blown Kantianism.

But the idea of a necessary link between language and thought is suspect, at best. When I wake up in the morning, there are a number of things that I am thinking without envisioning any words or sentences. I go to the refrigerator and get an apple. In order to accomplish this, I don't need to conjure up any sentences or words like refrigerator or apple, but one would be hard pressed to argue that I'm not in any way thinking of those things.

With respect to postmodernity's influence on the notion of world view, then, we should remember the following. It seems clear that, no matter how loudly one shouts that world views are dead, much more is required to make that thought even worth entertaining as a viable notion. Not only so but, depending on how we define a world view, a very strong case could be made, in spite of Derrida's protestations to the contrary, that what we have in the postmodern mind (or minds) is yet another example of a world-construct that is meant to be propagated among the masses. So, in the end, the idea of a world view is in no danger. Paraphrasing Mark Twain, the rumors of its death are highly exaggerated.

If we had the time, it would be worth our while pursuing the influence of this kind of postmodernity in certain theological circles: John Franke's *The Character of Theology* comes initially to mind. Without giving those views a fair hearing, suffice it to repeat at this point that he who marries the spirit of the age will soon find himself a widower.

REFORMED WORLD VIEW AS COVENANTAL WORLD VIEW

So how do we approach the subject of a Reformed World View? Some of you will know that there have been significant discussions over this as well. Just to use one example, the Dutch philosopher Herman Dooyeweerd, attempting to follow in the footsteps of Abraham Kuyper, worked out a detailed and often dense articulation of the notion of theoretical thought. Dooyeweerd contended that there must be a basic and fundamental distinction made between a philosophy, on the one hand, and a world view, on the other. Philosophy was concerned with matters theoretical, while a world view was itself *pre*-theoretical; it belonged to the domain of so-called "naïve experience."

I am personally not convinced that Dooyeweerd's distinctions are particularly helpful. Specifically, it seems to me that there is significant overlap, if not outright identity, between one's philosophy and one's world view. Granted that one's philosophy or world view can be more or less conscious and more or less articulated, there seems to me to be such a strong coincidence of subject matter that it is best to see world view and philosophy as on the same continuum. The distinction between theoretical and pre-theoretical, or naïve experience, seems to be one of emphasis and interest rather than of absolute principle.

For the Reformed Christian, a world view is informed by and must be consistent with Reformed theology. That is, just as philosophy is meant to be in the service of theology, so also world view is meant to be in the service of theology. It is meant to be that which is informed by, and built upon, our understanding of Scripture and the theology that flows from that. So, the natural question then becomes, "what particular aspects of Reformed theology are central to a Reformed world view?" In attempting to give an initial answer to this question, I would like to highlight two overarching Reformed theological tenets that must inform any and every Reformed world view. Following that I would like to interject one other aspect of our theology that is sometimes overlooked, but that must itself be seen to be more central to a Reformed world view than is sometimes thought.

PRINCIPIA AND COVENANT

It is likely that at least one of the main reasons that the concept of world view gained such prominence in the latter nineteenth and early twentieth centuries is that during this time there was a sea change in the way in which Christianity was viewed. With the insurgence of liberalism in the churches, and from there into the culture, some perceived a need to re-insert the basic picture of orthodoxy--the way in which orthodox Christianity had viewed the world in the past and should view it presently.

As an entry way into our theological discussion and its relationship to a Reformed world view, we should note a couple of Reformed pioneers whose emphases need particular attention. Enter James Orr (1844-1913). It was his book, *The Christian View of God and the World*, in which Orr began to think in terms of a world view. While it may be difficult to see how radical this was, we should remember that hardly any Christian was thinking or writing in these specific terms during this time. His beginning to work through a notion of world view put Orr almost alone in his defense of Christianity.

Orr's interest in world view was a result of his expertise in German theology and philosophy. The more he read of the German literature, the more he encountered the word *Weltanschauung* and related concepts. What struck him, as a pastor and apologist, was just how neatly Christianity fit into the concerns of those who were attempting to develop a conceptual worldview. Because Christianity, as truth, is a coherent system of truth, it (and Orr will argue, it alone) can address the concerns that are a part of world view thinking. Orr was convinced that nothing less than the comprehensive truth of Christianity could answer the attacks and critiques that were prevalent in his day.

Particularly important to Orr, we should note, was his emphasis on the opposition of *principles* or *principia*. So, says Orr,

> The opposition which Christianity has to encounter is no longer confined to special doctrines or to points of supposed conflict with the natural sciences,...but extends to the whole manner of conceiving of the world, and of man's place in it, the manner of conceiving of the entire system of things, natural and moral, of which we form a part. *It is no longer an opposition of detail, but of principle.* This circumstance necessitates an equal extension of the line of the defense. It is the Christian view of things in general which is attacked, and it is by an exposition and vindication of the Christian view of things as a whole that the attack can most successfully be met. [3]

There would be no effective defense of Christianity if it was done piecemeal, contended Orr. Christianity had to be defended as an entire *system* of thought and of life. We notice particularly that Orr contends that the opposition which Christianity faces is an opposition of *principle*. As we will see in a moment, a technical use of this term is important to keep in mind in these discussions. By 'principle' here is not meant simply a rule for behavior, or a particular belief.

From Scotland to the Netherlands

As most of us are aware, Abraham Kuyper was calling for precisely the same emphasis as was Orr. Kuyper, as Orr had done,

[3]   James Orr, *The Christian View of God and the World* (repr., Grand Rapids: Kregel, 1989), 4.

proposed that a proper defense of Christianity must consist of an all-encompassing approach. So, he says,

> If the battle is to be fought with honor and with hope of victory then *principle must be arrayed against principle*; then it must be felt that in Modernism the vast energy of an all embracing life-system assails us, then also it must be understood that we have to take our stand in a life-system of equally comprehensive and far-reaching power. And this powerful life-system is not to be invented nor formulated by ourselves, but is to be taken and applied as it presents itself in history.[4]

Now, it is this notion of *principle* that is at the root of a Reformed theology and world view. In order to understand the importance of this term, it is necessary for us to recall the deep-seated roots of the theological (and philosophical) notion of *principia*.[5]

The term *principia* has its roots in the Greek term *arche*, which means a beginning point, a source, or a first principle. Its theoretical roots go back at least as far as Aristotle, who argued that all *archai* or first principles or beginning points, are the "first point from which a thing either is or comes to be or is known...."[6] In other words, *archai*, according to Aristotle, provide the bedrock foundation for everything that is, or is known. In *Metaphysics* IV.3, Aristotle notes that first principles, in order to be *first* principles, must themselves be most certain, indemonstrable, immediately evident, and *never* a postulate or hypothesis. According to Aristotle, first principles are that which anyone must have when he comes to study anything at all. First principles, therefore, cannot be something that someone acquires in the midst of one's reasoning or argument. This concept of a beginning point, what some have called an Archimedean point, is a necessary and crucial aspect of *all* thinking and being. Aristotle understood this, philosophy has continued to articulate this idea, and Christian theology has seen it as basic to its own discipline.

In this sense, the *principia* that form the foundation for everything else are themselves transcendental in nature. They provide for the possibility of anything else: if in a particular science, then they provide for the possibility of that science. But if in an ultimate sense, as is the

---

[4] Abraham Kuyper, *Lectures on Calvinism* (1931; Grand Rapids: William B. Eerdmans Publishing Co., 1978), 11-12, emphasis mine.

[5] Here I depend heavily on the historical spade-work of Richard Muller.

[6] Quoted in Richard A. Muller, *Post-Reformation Reformed Dogmatics : Prolegomena to Theology*, (Grand Rapids: Baker Books, 1987), 1:431.

case with theological *principia*, then they provide for the possibility of anything else whatsoever. They provide for the possibility of *being* and for the possibility of *knowing*.

To use just one example in theology, the Dutch Reformed theologian Sibrandus Lubbertus argued in the late 16th century that all disciplines, and especially theology, require *principia*, and that such *principia* partake of the at least the following properties: (1) they are necessarily and immutably true, and

(2) they must be known *per se*, that is, in themselves, as both immediate and indemonstrable.[7]

By 'immediate' here is meant that the status of a *principium* is not taken from something external to it, but is inherent in the thing itself. It does not mean, strictly speaking, that nothing *mediates* the truth therein, but rather that nothing *external* mediates that truth.

By 'indemonstrable' here is meant that the *fact* of a *principium* is not proven by way of syllogism or by external means, but is such that it provides the ground upon which any other fact or demonstration depends. For example, *speaking of the discipline of theology*, Philippe du Plessis Mornay, the so-called "Hugenot Pope," states: "For if every science has its *principles*, which it is not lawful to remove, be it ever so little: much more reason is it that it should be so with that thing which hath the ground of all *principles* as its *principle*."[8]

What Mornay writes is not unique among the orthodox Reformed. Not only was he saying that theology has its own *principia*, but much more than that. He was also affirming that, whereas all sciences have their own *principia*, theology's *principia* under gird and underlie any and all other *principia*. The *principia* of other sciences are relative to those sciences; the *principia* of theology are prior to any other *principia* of any and all other disciplines. According to Richard Muller, "Divinity alone begins with the absolute first principles of things which depend on no other matters; whereas the basic principles of the other

---

[7] Ibid.

[8] Philippe du Plessis-Mornay, *A Worke Concerning the Trunesse of Christian Religion, Written in French: Against Atheists, Epicures, Paynims, Iewes, Mahumetists, and Other Infidels. By Philip of Mornay Lord of Plessie Marlie. Begunne to Be Translated into English by That Honourable and Worthy Gentleman, Syr Philip Sidney Knight, and at His Request Finished by Arthur Golding. Since Which Time, It Hath Bene Reviewed, and Is Now the Third Time Published, and Purged from Sundrie Faultes Escaped Heretofore, Thorow Ignorance, Carelesnes, or Other Corruption*, trans. Sir Philip Sidney Knight and Arthur Golding (London: George Eld, 1604), 2.

sciences are only first relative to the science for which they provide the foundation, the basic principles of theology are prior to any other 'principle of Being' or 'principle of knowing.'"[9]

It should be noted that this acknowledgment and development of *principia* during the sixteenth and seventeenth centuries had its focus within two primary disciplines - philosophy and theology. In philosophy, the concern had its focus in the thought and philosophy of Renee Descartes. For all that separated Cartesian philosophy from Reformed theology - and there was much that did - the concern for *principia* was paramount in both disciplines. Descartes' wanted his *principia* to be clear and distinct ideas concerning first the self, and then God, ideas that would provide the transcendental foundation for everything else that could be known.

For the Reformed, on the other hand, *principia* could never be located, even tangentially, in the human self. To do so would lead to the kind of scepticism that followed in the wake of Cartesian philosophy. Instead, as Muller notes,

> ...the classical philosophical language of *principia* was appropriated by the Reformed orthodox at a time and in a context where...[it] served the needs both of the Reformation sense of the priority of Scripture and the Reformation assumptions concerning the ancillary status of philosophy and the weakness of human reason. By defining both Scripture and God as principial in the strictest sense -- namely as true, immediate, necessary, and knowable... -- the early orthodox asserted the priority of Scripture over tradition and reason and gave conceptual status to the notion of its self-authenticating character in response to both Roman polemicists and philosophical skeptics of the era.[10]

This "priority of Scripture" that Muller mentions is at the heart of a distinctive Reformed world view and it may help us to recall that this is the context in which the Westminster Confession was written. Because the issue of authority was paramount at the time of the Reformation and in the Counter-Reformation, the Council of Trent thought it necessary both to enumerate the books of Scripture and to designate Jerome's Latin Vulgate as the "official" version of Scripture. You will know that the list of books enumerated by Trent is different from that given in the Westminster Confession.

---

[9] Muller, *Post-Reformation Reformed Dogmatics : Prolegomena to Theology*, 436.
[10] Ibid., 432.

What should be underscored here is that the issue is not simply that Protestants' canon of Scripture differs from the Romanists'. That is true enough. But what should be seen, and what is more fundamental in terms of our discussion of a Reformed world view, is that the Council of Trent determined, not only which books would be counted as Scripture *simpliciter*, but also asserted that the Roman church would *itself* be *canon*; that is, the Romanist church determined *itself*, through its decrees, to be the normative rule of faith and practice. So the issue is not simply which books are included in the canon: the issue is *why* particular books are included. For the Romanists, the ones included are there because the church says so.

It is not the case, therefore, that Scripture is the *principium* for the Roman church. Rather, with regard to the formal principle of the Reformation, two vastly different notions of *principium cognoscendi* (a principle or foundation of understanding) emerged. The Roman view is that holy mother church, and it alone, is the true, immediate and indemonstrable *principium*. This is why a *fides implicitas* implicit faith) is the proper response of those within that church, both to its interpretation of Scripture and tradition. For Protestants, however, Scripture, being inspired and self-attesting, provides its own criteria for canon, and thus is its own, self-referential, self-authenticating, authority.

This remind us of the point articulated in Chapter 1, section four of the Westminster Confession. After establishing the *necessity* of Scripture in section 1 and the *content* of Scripture in sections 2 and 3, section 4 declares, in no uncertain terms, the self-referential and self-attesting *authority* of Holy Scripture: "The authority of the Holy Scripture, for which it ought to be believed, and obeyed, dependeth not upon the testimony of any man, or Church; but wholly upon God (who is truth itself) the author thereof: and therefore it is to be received, because it is the Word of God" (WCF 1.4).

One of the first things that must be firmly embedded in our minds with respect to the *principium cognoscendi* is the absolute self-attesting authority of Scripture. Without doubt, some of the reasons for that are clear, particularly considering opposition from Roman Catholicism.

Notice first of all, that the divines are interested specifically in the authority of Scripture, and the intent of the paragraph is to set out for us the ground or reason why the Scriptures are *authoritative*, and thus why they ought to be believed and obeyed. The divines set out very clearly that the authority of Scripture does, in no way, rest on the Church or its councils, or on any man. Rather, its authority rests on its author, God, and is to be received because it is His Word. This is sometimes called the αυτοπιστον of Scripture, translated as self-attesting, or self-authenticating.

We should be clear here that self-attestation *does not* mean self-evident. Self-authentication, or attestation, is an objective attribute, whereas self-evident refers more specifically to the knowing agent's discernment. It therefore does *not* mean that revelation as self-authenticated compels agreement. That which is self-authenticating can be denied. It *does* mean that it *needs* no other authority as confirmation in order to be justified and absolutely authoritative in what it says. Nor does this mean that nothing else attends that authority; there are other evidences, as section five of chapter one clearly elucidate. What it *does* mean is that nothing else whatsoever is needed, nor is anything else able to supersede this ground in order for Scripture to be deemed authoritative.

This is why we must understand the nature of a *principium* in order to perceive on what a Reformed world view must rest. Again, according to Muller,

> Since...it is of the very nature of a first principle that it is most certain, indemonstrable or immediately evident, and never a postulate or hypothesis, the Reformed orthodox identification of Scripture as the *principium cognoscendi unicum* (single basis of understanding) of theology involves the assumption that the biblical norm cannot be rationally or empirically verified and, indeed, need not be -- and that its authority is known in and through its self-authenticating character.[11]

The Confession is quite clear here. When the question comes as to the ground or foundation of Scripture's authority, the Divines understood that to reference anything other than Scripture would be to deny the Word of God as theological *principium*. Also, note the juxtaposition of the two *principia* of theology embedded within this one section. The authority of Scripture depends on God who is truth itself, and therefore is to be received because it is His Word, not because *we* say it is His Word, or have shown it to be His Word, but because of what it *is*, the very Word of God.

It should be noted here that the point made in section four is not simply that Scripture is the Word of God because it says it is. Rather, the

---

[11]   Ibid., 436-437.

point is that Scripture is the Word of God because God, who is truth itself, is its author. This is an important point in the face of other, false, religions which also have books that claim to have come from God or to be his word. The divines were acquainted with such teachings and books which existed prior to the writing of this confession.

The point the Confession makes, however, is simply that God has worked in a particular way in history, revealing himself through various means along the way, and that now, since it has pleased him to commit such revelation to writing, he himself has authored Holy Scripture. It is incumbent on those who hear it or read it, therefore, to receive it because it is God Himself speaking in and through every word of it.

Two more clarifying points are necessary with respect to these *principia* to which we have already alluded: in Reformed thinking there were two *principia*; two categories were central. There was necessarily a *principium* with respect to Being and, just as necessarily, a *principium* with respect to knowing. *Principia*, therefore, refer primarily to the *principium essendi*, which is the principle, source or foundation of Being, and the *principium cognoscendi*, which is the principle, source, or foundation of knowing.

Given these two priorities, we readily see that what lies at the foundation of a Reformed world view are two primary doctrines, two *principia*—the doctrine of God and the doctrine of Scripture. Having looked at the first *principium*, a few important points should be mentioned concerning our doctrine of God, our *principium essendi*, and its importance for a Reformed world view.

The Ειμι

As we move from the necessity of Scripture as our *principium cognoscendi* to the necessity of God as our *principium essendi*, we need also to make clear just how our understanding of God provides for a Reformed world view. In order to do that, we must be clearer than perhaps we have been in the past. One of the things that we have been concerned to set forth in a Reformed articulation of theology, and thus of a world view, is the Creator/creature distinction. This vital point poses little problem it if is clearly defined. It means, in part, that as Reformed Christians, we affirm a two-level reality with respect to Being. This is in distinction from medieval theology, which argued, by and large, that because Being was a transcendental notion, and because, as a transcendental notion, it necessarily entails all that *is*, we simply cannot view creation as God's bringing about "more being."

In other words, medieval philosophers objected to the notion that, in creating God would have created more being. If such were the case, then God's infinity would not reach to his being, since 'more being' would *be* at the point of creation. "As they put it, God plus creatures = *plura entia, sed non plus entis*"(that is, more beings, but not more being).[12] This understanding seems to make it impossible to avoid univocal predication with respect to the Being of God and the being of creation. And, as Van Til has so forcefully taught us, if there is one moment of univocal predication with respect to God and creation, then the Creator/creature distinction is effectively erased.

In order to make clear just what kind of Creator/creature distinction is crucial to a Reformed world view, we should briefly examine Exodus 3:1-15.

> Now Moses was keeping the flock of his father-in-law, Jethro, the priest of Midian, and he led his flock to the west side of the wilderness and came to Horeb, the mountain of God. [2] And the angel of the LORD appeared to him in a flame of fire out of the midst of a bush. He looked, and behold, the bush was burning, yet it was not consumed. [3] And Moses said, "I will turn aside to see this great sight, why the bush is not burned." [4] When the LORD saw that he turned aside to see, God called to him out of the bush, "Moses, Moses!" And he said, "Here I am." [5] Then he said, "Do not come near; take your sandals off your feet, for the place on which you are standing is holy ground." [6] And he said, "I am the God of your father, the God of Abraham, the God of Isaac, and the God of Jacob." And Moses hid his face, for he was afraid to look at God.[7] Then the LORD said, "I have surely seen the affliction of my people who are in Egypt and have heard their cry because of their taskmasters. I know their sufferings, [8] and I have come down to deliver them out of the hand of the Egyptians and to bring them up out of that land to a good and broad land, a land flowing with milk and honey, to the place of the Canaanites, the Hittites, the Amorites, the Perizzites, the Hivites, and the Jebusites. [9] And now, behold, the cry of the people of Israel has come to me, and I have also seen the oppression with which the Egyptians oppress them. [10] Come, I will send you to Pharaoh that you may bring my people, the children of Israel, out of Egypt." [11] But Moses said to God, "Who am I that I should go to Pharaoh and

---

[12]   W. Norris Clarke, "Charles Hartshorne's Philosophy of God: A Thomistic Critique," in *Charles Hartshorne's Concept of God: Philosophical and Theological Responses*, ed. Santiago Sia (Dordrecht/Boston/London: Kluwer Academic Publishers, 1990), 108.

bring the children of Israel out of Egypt?" [12] He said, "But I will be with you, and this shall be the sign for you, that I have sent you: when you have brought the people out of Egypt, you shall serve God on this mountain." [13] Then Moses said to God, "If I come to the people of Israel and say to them, 'The God of your fathers has sent me to you,' and they ask me, 'What is his name?' what shall I say to them?" [14] God said to Moses, "I AM WHO I AM." And he said, "Say this to the people of Israel, 'I AM has sent me to you.'" [15] God also said to Moses, "Say this to the people of Israel, 'The LORD, the God of your fathers, the God of Abraham, the God of Isaac, and the God of Jacob, has sent me to you.' This is my name forever, and thus I am to be remembered throughout all generations.

There are a number of truths given to us in this text, some of which we cannot elaborate here. Nevertheless, at least three truths evident in this passage help us to see more clearly the superficiality of the minimized god of open theism. First, notice how God initially identifies himself to Moses: "And he said, 'I am the God of your father, the God of Abraham, the God of Isaac, and the God of Jacob.'"

The first way in which the LORD describes himself, is as *Moses'* God, the God of Moses' father, Abraham. This is phrasing is typically used throughout the Old Testament when God wants his people to know that he is *their* God (note Ex. 6:7, for example, as well as Jer. 7:23, 11:4, etc.). He identifies himself as the covenant God. Notice that just prior to this passage we read Exodus 2:24-25: "And God heard their groaning, and God remembered his covenant with Abraham, with Isaac, and with Jacob. God saw the people of Israel—and God knew."

The mention of Abraham, Isaac and Jacob is meant to remind us of God's relationship to his people, a people of his own choosing (John 15:16), a people for God's own possession (1 Peter 2:9). Exodus 3 opens with the reminder that God is a covenant God, and that he knew the sufferings of his people in Egypt.

When God appears to Moses in the burning bush, he announces himself as the God of the covenant by specifically identifying himself as Moses' God, and thus as the God of Israel. The passage is, therefore, replete with covenant language. Notice, Exodus 3:7, 9: "Then the LORD said, "I have surely seen the affliction of my people who are in Egypt and have heard their cry because of their taskmasters. I know their sufferings... And now, behold, the cry of the people of Israel has come to me, and I have also seen the oppression with which the Egyptians oppress them."

What God is actually saying to Moses is an elaboration of his initial announcement to him. He is telling Moses just what it means that he is a covenant God. There is an intensity about the language that communicates clearly that God is identifying himself with the suffering of his people. That intensity is communicated, in the first place, when God says that he has "surely seen" the suffering of his people.[13] In the second place, we are told twice (once in 2:25 and again in 3:7) that God knows the suffering of his people. In the context of God's covenant faithfulness to his people, it would be impossible to understand God's 'knowing' in these passages as something merely intellectual, as if God had learned something at a given point in the history of his people. The 'knowing' here is covenantal knowing. It is the kind of knowing, for example, that we see in Genesis 4:1, where Adam 'knew' Eve and she conceived. It is a knowing of identity, a knowing of intimacy, a knowing that highlights the union with the Knower of the ones known. So intimate is this knowing that the prophet Isaiah can say of the Lord himself, "...in all their affliction, he was afflicted" (see Isaiah 63:9ff.).

God comes to Moses, then, and announces two things: first, his covenantal status; he is a covenant-keeping God and as such he has identified himself with the suffering of his people. Moses has been chosen as God's instrument to deliver the Lord's people from their bondage.

The second thing to note in this text is that when Moses is called to the task of deliverer, he requests more information. He may have comprehended God's commitment to do what he said he would do, but he also realized that, if he was to be God's instrument, he would need to know as much as possible about the authority of the One who was sending him. So, he asked for God's name. He wanted to know what God is like, or exactly who it was sending him into Egypt. God replied to Moses, "I AM WHO I AM."

This revelation of God's name has prompted extensive discussion among commentators. Without reproducing the controversies surrounding this text, we should highlight a few points that are crucial for understanding what God reveals here.

The medieval view of this text was that God is revealing Himself here as the self-existent One. This is criticized by many contemporary Old Testament scholars on the grounds that concepts like the aseity of God would not have entered the mind of an ancient Israelite. But this

---

[13]   The intensity of the language is clearer in the original Hebrew.

certainly cannot be the case, given the history of God's dealings with his people. This interpretation speaks more about the influence of Immanuel Kant on current hermeneutics than about the text itself.

We should note, however, that, without question, in this text God declares his self-existence. Though he has initially announced himself as the God who is *with* his people, and thus *in* history, when he is asked to give his name, he announces himself as the God who is also above history: he alone is the "I AM."

One of the causes of some commentators' confusion about what God is saying here is their fascination with the etymology of the phrase, to the neglect of its revelational context. It is virtually impossible to discover by analysis of terms alone the significance of this divine name.

Rather than isolating the pronouncing of the divine name from the context in which it is revealed, we can properly understand it only within that very context. Yahweh does indeed reveal his divine independence. In the context of the Exodus narrative he proves himself to be unlimited, not constrained or limited by temporal categories. More generally, he announces himself as one who is independent of the created order and therefore sovereign over it. "I Am Who I Am" indicates that God possesses his existence without beginning, without end, without explanation beyond himself. The ultimate fact of divine revelation is that God is who he is, without cause, without beginning or end. Of God alone can it be said, "He is who he is." God is the "Eimi."[14] This revelation of God's name to Moses takes on such significance that it is used over 5000 times in Scripture. The announcement in Exodus 3 was clearly meant to resonate throughout the whole of Scripture. As Calvin notes, "...contrary to grammatical usage, [God] used the same verb in the first person as a substantive, annexing it to a verb in the third person; *that our minds may be filled with admiration as often as his incomprehensible essence is mentioned.*"[15]

This is precisely what was modeled for Moses by the event of divine revelation that was given with the verbal revelation. This "show and tell" method of God's revelation seems, too, to have been all too often under-emphasized. God often tells us who he is by giving us an earthly picture, or analogy, of who he is. It is not an insignificant detail

---

[14]   This is a transliteration of the Greek word, ειμι, translated as, "I Am."

[15]   Commentary on Exodus 3:14, quoted in Richard A. Muller, *Post-Reformation Reformed Dogmatics : The Rise and Development of Reformed Orthodoxy, Ca. 1520 to Ca. 1725: The Divine Essence and Attributes*, 2nd ed., vol. 3 (Grand Rapids, Mich.: Baker Books, 2002), 250, my emphasis.

that what draws Moses into God's presence is such a picture of who God is. There is no analogy in the creation for the independent and the uncreated. So God creates a picture of his character in the burning bush. The fire does not derive its burning from the context in which it burns. It is self-generated, contradicting all rules of creation. The bush is on fire, but the fire is not dependent on the bush; it possesses its own energy. This seems a deliberate and *revelational* sign given by God to unveil the significance both of God's covenantal revelation to Moses, and his revelation of the divine name—"I Am Who I Am."

We should see, then, that the *un*burning bush shows, on the one hand, the absolute independence of God, that he possesses being in and of himself in a manner that is without precedence in all of creation. It points to an ontological truth, this ultimate fact about God that makes the human mind stagger and reel, because we have no categories to describe or understand this element of the existence of God; that he simply is. But it also shows, on the other hand, that, while remaining the "I Am," while remaining *a se*, while remaining *God*, God is nevertheless *with* his people, just as the fire was *with* the bush. The significance of the bush that did not burn, was that, in any other circumstance, the fire would need the bush in order to be fire. Not only so, but in being used as fuel, the bush itself would be consumed by the fire. In what Moses saw, however, neither did the fire need the bush, nor was the bush consumed. The "I Am" has covenanted with his people; therefore as he abides with them they are not destroyed.

Here, then, is the beauty of God's character; it is the wonderful mystery of the God who is *a se*, eternally and immutably dependent on nothing but himself, covenanting with us, relating to us, in such a way that we can know and love him.

So there are two crucial and necessary aspects to our understanding of God: God in Himself, and God in relation to the world/His people. But in order to be clearer and more specific about a Reformed world view that is, in every sense of the word, *Christian*, we need to elaborate one further point, one that has to do with just *how* it is that this God who is the "I Am" relates Himself to his world.

It should not surprise us that it is at precisely this point where the Christian religion distinguishes itself from all others and from all other notions of God's relationship to the world. So it should not surprise us as well that it is at precisely this point, the point of God's relating himself to the world, where many go wrong with respect to a Creator/creature distinction. That distinction becomes blurred and fuzzy at just here.

Stephen Davis, to cite only one example, is a philosopher who claims to be a Christian. His world view includes a Creator/creature distinction, but he struggles to hold fast to a traditional understanding of who God is. In his defense of what he calls "temporal eternity," for example, he is convinced that the traditional understanding of eternity, in which God is not subject to time, serves, in the end, to deny the existence of the Christian God. He sets out the following three-point argument to illustrate his point:

(1) God creates x.
(2) x first exists at T.
(3) Therefore, God creates x at T.[16]

Given this argument, says Davis, a timeless God cannot create anything at all. He cannot create because, Davis argues, we do not have a usable concept of a temporal causation that would allow for these temporal statements (1 and 2) to be meaningful. So, says Davis, "...we are within our rights in concluding that [(1)] and [(2)] entail that God is temporal, i.e. that a timeless being cannot be the creator of the universe."[17]

Furthermore, says Davis, it is illegitimate to hold to the eternity of God because of the ways in which Scripture speaks of God. With respect to Scripture's depictions of God, Davis says this: "He makes plans. He responds to what human beings do, e.g. their evil deeds or their acts of repentance. He seems to have temporal location and extension. The Bible does not hesitate to speak of God's years and days... And God seems to act in temporal sequences—first he rescues the children of Israel from Egypt and later he gives them the Law...."[18]

We should note here that Davis' motive is to seek to do justice to the Christian view of God as he is presented to us in Scripture. He is not, like those who set forth atheological arguments, attempting to prove God's nonexistence. The price he pays for this worthy motive, however, is too high.

In order to try to safeguard the biblical language with respect to God and his activity in the world, Davis ends up denying him his rightful

---

[16]   Stephen T. Davis, "Temporal Eternity," in *Philosophy of Religion: An Anthology*, ed. Louis P. Pojman (Belmont, CA: Wadsworth/Thomson Learning, 2003), 211, my numbering.
[17]   Ibid., 213.
[18]   Ibid.

status as God.[19] In order to argue for God's essentially limited existence, he argues for a god that is contrary to the Triune God of Christianity. The god of which Davis writes is a "god" who is constrained by the (limited and dependent) duration of the temporal world. He is able to act *only* within such constraints. Clearly, the notion of One who exemplifies maximal greatness is absent here. Clearly the Christian God, as orthodox, Reformed Christianity has historically conceived him, is nowhere to be found.

Another example is William Lane Craig, arguably the most influential evangelical apologist today. In a book entitled, *Time and Eternity*, Craig wrestles with God's eternity relative to time. He asks the question of whether a personal God can stand in some kind of relationship to the world and, at the same time, not be constrained by time. His answer is alarming.

> Imagine once more God existing changelessly alone without creation, but with a changeless determination of His will to create a temporal world with a beginning. Since God is omnipotent, His will is done, and a temporal world comes into existence. Now this presents us with a dilemma. Either God existed prior to creation or He did not. Suppose He did. In that case, God is temporal, not timeless, since to exist *prior* to some event is to be in time. Suppose, then, that God did not exist prior to creation. In that case, without creation, He exists timelessly, since He obviously did not come into being along with the world at the moment of creation.
>
> This second alternative presents us with a new dilemma. Once time begins at the moment of creation, either God becomes temporal in virtue of His real relation to the temporal world or else He exists just as timelessly with creation as He does without it. If we choose the first alternative, then, once again, God is temporal. But what about the second alternative? Can God remain untouched by the world's temporality? It seems not. For at the first moment of time, God stands in a new relation in which He did not stand before (since there was no

---

[19]   As do many philosophers of religion who have found it necessary to give up on God's eternity. See also Nicholas Wolterstorff, "God Everlasting," in *God and the Good: Essays in Honor of Henry Stob*, ed. Henry Stob, Clifton Orlebeke, and Lewis B. Smedes (Grand Rapids, Michigan: William B. Eerdmans Publishing Co., 1975).; Richard Swinburne, *The Coherence of Theism*, Rev. ed. (Oxford, New York: Clarendon Press; Oxford University Press, 1993).

"before").[20]

Given these two examples, (and they could be easily and almost endlessly multiplied), it is incumbent on those of us who maintain a Creator/creature distinction to be clear as to our meaning. Just how *does* God go about relating himself to his universe? Here the church has struggled. From the side of evangelical Arminianism, the "solution" has been to make God in some way or ways essentially dependent on human choices. One of the reasons this position has had such enormous influence is, in part, because there are in fact passages in Scripture which squarely and unequivocally locate God in the space-time continuum, and which articulate a dependence of God on man for certain things to happen. So the Arminian position has had a forceful and tremendous following.

The Reformed view, on the other hand, will have no such dependence. The Reformed have maintained that it is God's aseity that takes precedence over any other aspect of God's character. But why think that passages that deal with God's being take precedence over others that deal with his relationship to creation? Muller gives us a clue as to why the Reformed scholastics understood things this way:

> Here, admittedly, the orthodox line of thought is guided not by a totally open or unbiased exegesis of texts, but by an *ontological conception* of the immutability of God: this guiding conception in turn leads to an interpretation of Scripture that gives priority to those texts stressing the unchangeability of God over those texts which indicate change, priority to those texts which stress God's otherness over those which indicate emotion, passion, or other kinship with humanity. But this is not a case of rationalism or metaphysical speculation overruling revelation: instead it is an example of one of the many instances in which theology must make a choice concerning its view of God, deciding which aspects of the scriptural view are governing concepts, anthropomorphisms or transcendence, the "repentance" of God or the divine constancy. And, in this case in particular, the Reformed orthodox stand not only in line of the more philosophical arguments typical of scholastic theology but, together with the older scholasticism, in the line of the church's exegetical tradition - and indeed, in accord with the

---

[20]   William Lane Craig, *Time and Eternity: Exploring God's Relationship to Time* (Wheaton, Illinois: Crossway Books, 2001), 86-87.

doctrinal statements and with the exegesis of the Reformers.[21]

But Reformed views of God's relationship to the world, in wanting to stress this "ontological priority" have themselves not always been able to maintain a biblical balance in attempting to describe God's relationship to the world. For example, Paul Helm, a Calvinistic philosopher, in attempting to explain Calvin, states:

> So the truth about atonement, about reconciliation to God, has to be represented to us as if it implied a change in God, and so an inconsistency, an apparent contradiction, in his actions towards us. But in fact there is no change in God; he loves us from eternity. There is however, a change in us, a change that occurs as by faith Christ's work is appropriated. *The change is not from wrath to grace, but from our belief that we are under wrath to our belief that we are under grace.*[22]

We have to ask the question, does this way of construing things really do justice to the biblical material? Does the notion of our being "under wrath" in Adam, and "under grace" in Christ really reduce to a subjective belief? Does this way of trying to safeguard God's ontological aseity and immutability skew the biblical data at significant points?

Note also how Calvin speaks of this relationship:

> What, therefore, does the word 'repentance' mean? Surely its meaning is like that of all other modes of speaking that describe God to us in human terms. For because our weakness does not attain to his exalted state, the description of him that is given to us must be accommodated to our capacity so that we may understand it. Now the mode of accommodation is for him to represent himself to us not as he is in himself, *but as he seems to us.* Although *he is beyond disturbance of mind*, yet he testifies that he is angry towards sinners. Therefore whenever we hear that God is angered, we ought not to imagine any emotion in him, but rather to consider that this expression has been taken from our own human experience; because God, whenever he is exercising judgment, *exhibits the appearance* of one kindled and angered.[23]

---

[21]   Muller, *Post-Reformation Reformed Dogmatics : The Rise and Development of Reformed Orthodoxy, Ca. 1520 to Ca. 1725: The Divine Essence and Attributes*, 451-452, my emphasis.
[22]   Paul Helm, *John Calvin's Ideas* (Oxford: Oxford University Press, 2004), 395, my emphasis.
[23]   John Calvin, *Institutes of the Christian Religion*, ed. John T. McNeill ; trans. Ford Lewis Battles; Library of Christian Classics (London: SCM Press, 1961), I.17.12.

The Ἐιμί and Εἰκὼν

How do we respond to these ideas? It seems to me that such statements, in an attempt to give due weight to God's aseity, also serve to minimize or otherwise subdue the *real* relationship that God has with his creation, and with us as his image.

One way to think again about this relationship is given to us in Exodus 3, and is given its fullest expression thereafter. Remember what the Lord said to Moses in Exodus 3:8? Because he had seen his people's suffering, he said, "I have come down to deliver..." Now this principle of the Lord's condescension provides a clue to a proper understanding of God's relationship to his world, and thus to a proper understanding of the Creator/creature relationship.

Without rehearsing the covenant-historical data as it is given to us in Holy Scripture, it should be obvious to us that this "I have come down to deliver" statement of the Lord's in Exodus 3 reaches its climax in the Person of Jesus Christ. In other words, God's own illustration and explanation of how he can relate himself to his creation reaches its climactic expression in Emmanuel, God with us, the person of Jesus Christ. So, that which the burning bush was meant to symbolize - the aseity of God together with his covenant relationship - is seen most clearly in Christ himself.

Let us, then, take seriously the fact that our Christology organizes our understanding of God's "relationality." How, specifically, does the person of Christ help us to understand who God is and how he relates to us? How does the person of Christ organize our understanding of the Creator/creature relationship?

Without working through a detailed exegesis of all the relevant texts, *orthodox* Christology has always understood the Person of Christ in a particular way. We can briefly elaborate on that understanding by looking more closely at Philippians 2:5-8.[24] First, the passage: "Have this mind among yourselves, which is yours in Christ Jesus, who, though he

---

[24]   We should recognize at the outset that we do not do justice to this passage by concentrating on its Christology. The point the apostle is attempting to make *by way of Christology* is a point about our own sanctification; he is wanting us to model the behavior exemplified in Christ, specifically the behavior that culminated in Christ's incarnation. Given our present concerns, however, we will focus our attention on the Christology at hand.

was in the form of God, did not count equality with God a thing to be grasped, but made himself nothing, taking the form of a servant, being born in the likeness of men. And being found in human form, he humbled himself by becoming obedient to the point of death, even death on a cross." This has been a controversial passage, not so much because of what it says, as we will see, but because of what it has often been thought to say. There are two central ideas present in this text that relate to our concerns and that have been the focus of various controversies. We will see, however, that these ideas serve to confirm what orthodox Christology has historically affirmed. Those two ideas are 'form (*morph'ē*) of God,' and 'made himself nothing (*ekenōsen*).'[25]

What, then, does Paul mean when he says that Christ was 'in the form' of God? We should first note that the word translated 'form' is used only here in the entirety of Scripture.[26] For that reason, the determination of its meaning finds its *locus* within its immediate context.[27] We should also note that the word itself is characterized by a broad range of meanings, making the immediate context all the more important.[28]

Within the context, we find two markers that help us understand what Paul is telling us. The first marker is the correspondence that is apparent between Paul's phrase 'form of God' and the phrase 'equality with God.' Whatever one makes of the differences between these two phrases, there can be little question that the two are meant to point to the same reality, and that the one helps us see the meaning of the other. According to Silva, "...it would be a grave mistake to ignore Käsemann's point that in the literature of the Hellenistic religions *morphē theou* and *isotheos physis* 'are parallel and even become synonymous.'"[29] Paul's notion of Christ being in the form of God, therefore, is tantamount to the notion of equality. Being in the form of God means being equal to God.

The second marker that helps us see something of Paul's meaning in this passage lies in the parallel phrase 'form of a servant'

---

[25] There other phrases and words in this context that offer some difficulty exegetically, among which is, for example, Paul's speaking of Christ as not considering his own position as 'a thing to be grasped' (*harpagmon*).

[26] With the possible exception of Mark 16:12.

[27] This is the case for all words, but is even more important exegetically with *hapax legomena*.

[28] Moisés Silva, *Philippians*, ed. Kenneth Barker, The Wycliffe Exegetical Commentary (Chicago: Moody Press, 1988), 115.. For the notion of semantic extension, see also Moisés Silva, *Biblical Words and Their Meaning: An Introduction to Lexical Semantics* (Grand Rapids, Michigan: Zondervan Publishing House, 1983), 77.

[29] Silva, *Philippians*, 114.

(*morphē doulou*). What Paul has in mind in using this phrase is itself further explained by the 'likeness of men.'

The word 'form' in this passage, therefore, is chosen by Paul, in part, in order to communicate two analogous, though not identical, situations.[30] The 'form of God' is further explained as Christ being equal to God. But, as we noted above, Paul is not *immediately* concerned in this passage to give us a Christian-theistic ontology. He is concerned to present to us the quintessential example of how we as the Lord's people are to think and live. The second use of 'form,' then, refers, not so much to the being of Christ himself, but to his status as incarnate. In that case, 'form' is used to express the role that Christ agreed to when he agreed to be 'born in the likeness of men.'

The clear and initial implication of this text is that the preincarnate Son of God, as the second person of the Trinity, determined voluntary to come down in such a way that he would identify himself with humanity. He came by taking on our likeness and by taking the role of a servant of the Lord. According to Fee, therefore, the word 'form' (*morphē*) can be best understood as "*that which truly characterizes a given reality.*"[31]

What then does Paul mean when he says that this preincarnate Son, who was in the form of God but who took on the form of a servant 'made himself nothing?' Here controversy has raged, especially since, in some translations, the phrase is (properly) translated as 'emptied himself' (NASB). Paul explains to us what he means when he notes that this self-negation, whatever it is, had to do with the fact that the Christ did not count his own equality with God 'a thing to be grasped.'

Whenever ambiguous words are employed, the only proper method of discovery lies in the (less ambiguous) context in which those words appear. The force of what Paul is saying, therefore, should not rest on a supposed resolution to the ambiguity, but, if possible, on clearer signs along the way. In this context and because of it, the meaning of the passage is quite clear.

We are, says Paul, to cultivate within ourselves the same mind-set that Christ himself had when he chose to come down to us. More specifically, we are to do "nothing from rivalry or conceit, but in

---

[30] Again, given the semantic extension of the term, it is the perfect term to use in this case.
[31] Gordon D. Fee, "Philippians," in *The New International Commentary on the New Testament*, ed. Ned B. Stonehouse, F. F. Bruce, Gordon D. Fee (Grand Rapids, Michigan: William B. Eerdmans Publishing Company, 1995), 204.

humility count others more significant than yourselves" (Phil. 2:3). We are not, then, to hold onto whatever status or position we think we might own or be ours by right, but rather to consider that the position or status of others is more significant.

In this light, and because of this context, it becomes clearer just what Paul is saying about our Savior. In his decision to take on the likeness of humanity, he did not simply look to his own position and status, nor did he count that position and status something that he should, in every way, hold onto. Rather he considered the position and status of those who are lower, who could not reach up to his position, and he determined to stoop down to their level, for their sake.

We should be clear here. Paul is emphatically *not* saying that the reason the Son of God became man was because of something intrinsic in us. Christ did not come because we deserved it, or because there was something in us that motivated his coming. Rather, Paul is pointing out to us the depth and breadth of humility as it is expressed in the decision of the Son of God to become man. He is explaining to us just what humility and even humiliation are. It is the decision to give up what may be rightfully ours for the sake of others. It is to be *for* someone else rather than *for* oneself. It is, in a word, to be self*less*.

The ambiguous phrases, then, become clearer. It is not as though Christ emptied himself *of* something; that is not Paul's point. Paul's point is that Christ emptied *himself* by becoming something that he was not previously, something that, by definition, required humility and, ultimately, humiliation (Phil. 2:8). For Christ to make himself nothing, says Paul, is for him to humble himself, and he humbles himself by being born in the likeness of men, and by becoming obedient to the point of death. The self-emptying is, in point of fact, a self-*adding*. Hence Turretin:

> Here also belongs the verb *ekenōse*, which is not to be taken simply and absolutely (as if he ceased to be God or was reduced to a nonentity, which is impious even to think concerning the eternal and unchangeable God), but in respect of state and comparatively because he concealed the divine glory under the veil of flesh and as it were laid it aside; not by putting off what he was, but by assuming what he was not.[32]

---

[32]   Francis Turretin, *Institutes of Elenctic Theology*, ed. James T. Dennison Jr, trans. George Musgrave Giger, (Phillipsburg, New Jersey: Presbyterian and Reformed Publishing Company, 1994), 2:314. Though it cannot be pursued here, it is instructive to

We see this principle displayed for us, albeit in nascent form, in the Old Testament as well. We remember Moses' bold request that the Lord display the fullness of his glory to Moses (Ex. 33:18). This, Moses was told, would be certain death. Instead, the Lord, in his mercy, did show Moses his glory, but only as veiled; Moses could only glimpse the back side of the LORD as he passed by the cleft of the rock in which Moses was hidden. Was the LORD less than fully God as he passed by Moses? Certainly not. His proclamation as he passed by, what Luther called the "Sermon on the Name" was meant to remind Moses that the "I Am" was present. Rather he was accommodating himself to Moses in a way that demonstrated both his glory (The LORD, the LORD...) as well as the veiling of the fullness of that glory. The LORD came down, and showed himself to, even as he hid himself from, Moses.

The 'Emmanuel' principle in Philippians should therefore be obvious. Christ made a decision, choosing humiliation. It was not necessary for him to decide to humble himself; he had every right to continue without adding to himself the humiliating status of humanity. But he determined not to. The one who is equal to God, who is in the form of God, who is himself God (John 1:1), did not stop being God (such a thing would be impossible), but rather he took on something that was not a part of him previously. He took on human nature (John 1:14).

Clearly, it is not as though he relinquished deity in order to become man. This pattern is nowhere given in Scripture; it is, in fact, an impossibility. Rather, just as the 'I Am' remains LORD while, at the same time, coming down to be the God of Abraham, Isaac and Jacob, so the second Person of the Trinity remains God, while coming down to be the God-man. This *is* the covenant, as the Westminster Confession reminds us. Christ is the *substance* of the covenant (WCF 7:6, WLC 35; cf. Col. 2:8ff.).

The Christology we have been delineating here, as we have said, is nothing new. Any cursory survey of the church's position on the hypostatic union will bring out the same points. Moreover, the position

---

note that Turretin links an understanding of the Trinity to an understanding of the hypostatic union: "For as in the Trinity, the unity of essence does not hinder the persons from being distinct from each other and their properties and operations from being incommunicable, so the union of natures in the person of Christ does not prevent both the natures and their properties from remaining unconfounded and distinct" (311). The serious point to be made here is that a confusion or ignorance, or worse, denial, of the orthodox notion of Christology could imply the same with respect to the Trinity, such that Christianity could be replaced for another religion altogether.

of the Chalcedonian Creed is ample evidence that this is the church's historical position on Christology. That Creed reminds us that the incarnation has never been regarded as God's abandoning of any of his attributes at all. Rather, it is in the incarnation that we begin to see how it is that God can relate to his creation, without becoming less than God. The Creed affirms that the Son of God, as God, is to be "acknowledged in two natures inconfusedly (ασυγχυτως), unchangeably (ατρεπτως), indivisibly (αδιαιρέτως), and inseparably (αχωρίστως)." The Creed goes on to affirm, concerning this hypostatic union, that with regard to these two natures, "the distinction of natures [is] by no means taken away by the union, but rather the property of each nature [is] preserved, and concurring in one Person and one Subsistence, not parted or divided into two persons, but one and the same Son, and only begotten, God the Word, the Lord Jesus Christ...."[33]

If we take the Chalcedonian Creed seriously (and the church, both Catholic and Protestant, has done so since the Creed was written), then the theological priorities of our thinking in this matter become clearer to us. First, we should be clear about the fact that there are two crucial concepts in the Creed, and thus in our thinking about God and his relationship to us, that define the parameters of how we are to understand God's accommodation to us. Those two concepts are 'person' and 'nature.'

To the extent that God takes on the nature of created reality, to that extent must *he* be subject to (certain aspects of) creation. Historically, however, in orthodox theology, priority has always been given to 'person' over against 'nature.' This is so because what belongs to 'person' is independent and individuated in a way that what belongs to nature is not. God's accommodation presupposes that he *was*, and was (Triune) *person*, before coming down to the created level. It is for this reason, it seems to me, that theology has historically attempted to delineate just who God is, quite apart from his accommodation, in order thereafter to explain God's accommodation itself. God, as we have seen in the Old Testament, or the second *person* of the Trinity, as we see more clearly in the New, *is* a person with distinct characteristics and attributes,

---

[33] It is worth noting here that open theists seem not to have seen the profound implications of this. They seem mired in a kind of theological Eutychianism, in which there is no way that God can take on another nature until and unless he abandons (at least part of) his own.

prior to his accommodation to and with his creation.[34]

While there are careful distinctions here that must be maintained with respect to God (e.g., that God's essence is identical with God himself), there is absolutely no question that what orthodox Christology has always taught is that God came down, in the second person of the Trinity, who was and remains fully God, and he took on a human nature without thereby in any way changing his essential deity. This was brought out more clearly during the period of the Reformation in which the so-called *extra calvinisticum* is charged to Calvinists by the Lutherans. Without going into the details, it is worth noting that it was the Reformed, not the Lutherans, who insisted that the Person of the Son of God was not, indeed *could not be*, contained within the Incarnate Christ. The *"extra"* to which this refers is the deity of the Son of God which, while characterizing the person of Christ, nevertheless transcends his human nature. To think that because God interacts with creation he must change his essential nature or in some way limit his essential deity, is, in effect, to fail to see the Incarnation for what it is, according to the Reformed. While we cannot comprehend just what it means for one Person fully to possess two distinct natures, we must affirm it in order for the gospel, in its fullest biblical sense from Genesis to Revelation, to be what it is.[35]

CONCLUSION

What we have been urging here, therefore, is that a Reformed world view be a full-orbed *Christian* world view. It is not enough simply to acknowledge a Creator/creature relationship; it is not enough simply to be theists. We are, and must acknowledge, *Christian* theism as the only alternative available; without it, no proper view of the world is possible. If our world view is going to be Christian, and Reformed Christian, then

---

[34] As Turretin notes, a person or hypostasis is an "intellectual *suppositum*," having its own incommunicable existence. A person participates in a nature, which itself (on the created level at any rate) is communicable. For the best summary of this terminology, albeit in a Trinitarian context, see Richard A. Muller, *Post-Reformation Reformed Dogmatics : The Rise and Development of Reformed Orthodoxy, Ca. 1520 to Ca. 1725: The Triunity of God*, vol. 4. (Grand Rapids, Michigan: Baker Book House, 2003), esp. 167-195.

[35] It strikes me that one of the root problems with so-called "open theism" is that it is, in the end, more rationalistic than the very 'Hellenists' it seeks to oppose. To maintain that, in order to relate to creation God must essentially change, is to deny the unfathomable mystery that just *is* 'God with us.'

we must take seriously the two bedrock *principia* of Reformed thinking: the absolute self-attesting Scripture, and the God of Scripture who reveals himself preeminently and climactically in the person of Jesus Christ.

And now we have come full circle from where we began. It was James Orr who was most insistent that any *Christian* view of God and the world would have to encompass the Incarnation as its central focus. So, says Orr,

> ...if Christianity is not to be parted with, its full testimony to itself must be maintained... Formerly it was shown that the attempts to maintain Christianity, while rejecting the truth of the Incarnation, have uniformly failed. Now we have seen why it is so. ...Thus it is that the Lord stands constantly challenging the ages to give their answer to His question, "What think ye of Christ? whose Son is He?" and increasingly it is shown that it is not in the world's power to put this question aside. However silenced for the moment, it soon again asserts its rights, and will not cease to be heard till humanity, from one end of the earth to the other, has joined in the devout acknowledgment—"My Lord and my God.[36]

We have not engaged important and significant discussions of Christianity and its relationship to the arts, to culture generally, and to other aspects of a world view. What we have done instead is seek to ground any of those discussions in the necessity of Christ for a Reformed world view. The necessity of Christ turns us immediately to the necessity of revelation, and therefore back to the two *principia* that provide the foundation and ground for any discussion of a *Reformed* view of the world.

---

[36]   Orr, *The Christian View of God and the World,* 234-235.

Chapter 2

Claiming Every Inch: The Worldview of Abraham Kuyper

James Edward McGoldrick[1]

When in 1880 the Free University of Amsterdam opened for classes, its founder Abraham Kuyper delivered the inaugural address in which he asserted, "there is not an inch in the entire domain of…human life of which Christ, who is sovereign of all, does not proclaim 'Mine.'"[2]

Creation of the Free University marked a public commitment of Reformed Christians to implement in education their belief that *all truth is God's truth,* an assertion they believed made necessary by the growth of secularism as the dominant worldview in Dutch society. The basis of education in the new university was to be "faith in God's Word objectively infallible in Scripture and subjectively offered…by the Holy Spirit." This was to be a "line of demarcation" distinguishing the Free University from public institutions of higher learning where opposition

---

[1]   James McGoldrick PhD is retired Professor of History from Cedarville University and currently teaches part-time in the Greenville Presbyterian Theological Seminary. Dr. McGoldrick is ordained in the Presbyterian Church in America.
[2]   Abraham Kuyper, *Souvereiniteit in Eigen Kring,* trans. Wayne A. Kobes (Amsterdam: J. H. Kruyt, 1880), 35. An abbreviated English translation appears in *Abraham Kuyper: A Centennial Reader* (hereafter *Centennial Reader),* ed. James D. Bratt (Grand Rapids William B. Eerdmans Publishing Company, 1998), 461-90.

to historic Christianity prevailed.[3]   The Christian university was to be free from state control and, therefore, at liberty to conduct *its* research and teaching within the framework of a biblical worldview. Kuyper maintained that Christians must have a comprehensive view of all of life from a Scriptural perspective, which is the basis for their choices and informs all their actions. It deals with the most fundamental issues of life: *Where did we come from? Why are we here? Where are we going? How do we get there?*

In opposition to the naturalist-secularist modern worldview, Abraham Kuyper declared humanity and all of creation to be in an *abnormal* condition because of sin. This is particularly evident in the noetic effects of sin which pollute human minds and prevent them from achieving the proper understanding of themselves. As a consequence, they divide life into religious and secular categories, an egregious error caused by their abnormal condition, that is, they are "dead in trespasses and sins" (Eph. 2:1). In Kuyper's words, lost sinners have "all the properties belonging to a corpse."[4] He maintained there are " two kinds of people. Both are human, but one is inwardly different from the other,…thus they face the *cosmos* from different points of view and are impelled by different impulses. [This means there are] two kinds of human life and two kinds of science [scholarship]."[5]

A biblical worldview is necessarily antithetical to all competing views in every domain of life. Kuyper and his colleagues at the Free University applied this principle of antithesis in education, philosophy, law, science, etc., and concluded there could be no compromise with unbelief. [6]

Kuyper became Holland's most vigorous proponent of Reformed orthodoxy, but he did not begin his labors as a minister with that conviction. A brilliant student from childhood, he followed his father into the ministry of the Dutch Reformed Church, after graduating from the University of Leyden as a Doctor of Theology. While engaged in preparation for his career, Kuyper uncritically accepted the rationalistic approach to theology, which had become the routine method of

---

[3]   Ibid., 486.

[4]   Abraham Kuyper, *Calling and Repentance* (available on line at http://the-highway.com/calling-repentance_Kuyper.html).

[5]   Abraham Kuyper, *Principles of Sacred Theology,* trans. J. H. DeVries (1898; repr., Grand Rapids: Baker Book House, 1980), 154.

[6]   John M. Frame, *Cornelius Van Til: an Analysis of His Thought* (Phillipsburg, NJ: P&R Publishing, 1995), 22, 188.

instruction in all public universities in the Netherlands. Years after his conversion he related that he had begun his pastoral work while yet in an unbelieving state, and he praised God for the witness of parishioners at the village church in Beesd who recognized his plight and prayerfully sought his salvation. Miss Pietje Baltus, for example, challenged her pastor's failure to preach gospel truth and testified to him of the grace of God in her own life. She presented Kuyper with the historic confessions of their church and convinced him to read John Calvin's *Institutes of the Christian Religion,* a work his professors had ridiculed.

Although the learned pastor tried to rebut Miss Baltus and other orthodox critics of his ministry, he soon relented and began listening carefully to their appeals. By the grace of God, the witness of those common people without academic credentials became the human means to bring the skeptical Kuyper to Christ and to transform him into a defender of the faith he once scorned.

At the close of his three-year ministry in Beesd, Kuyper moved to Utrecht to join the pastoral staff at the *Domkerk,* the leading congregation of the National Church in that city. This church had a reputation for orthodoxy, but its leaders were poorly prepared to confront the challenges from liberal theologians, and some of them timidly avoided controversies. Kuyper, however, soon called for an energetic defense of the historic Reformed faith. As he said, "we cannot be passive and silent toward those who reject God's Word and our holy faith."[7] By taking that position, Kuyper placed himself in an antagonistic relationship to leaders of the Dutch Reformed Church and their political benefactors in the civil government. His aspiration was to cleanse the state church of false teaching and to emancipate it from dependence upon state financial support. He described his aspirations this way: "for my own sake and for others, the restoration of a church that could be our Mother had to be the goal of my life."[8]

The long road to reformation proved to be perilous, and in the end, unsuccessful, and by 1892 separation from the Dutch Reformed Church was the only honorable course remaining for believers of the Bible, a step they took as a last resort and with profound sorrow. Persecutions, which included arrests, fines, expulsions from the ministry, and loss of church properties, were the price they paid for loyalty to

---

[7]   The details of his conversion and subsequent defense of the Reformed faith are in his essay "Confidentially," in *Centennial Reader,* 45-61.
[8]   Ibid., 61.

God's Word.[9]

In order to assert Christ's lordship over the church that professed to serve his cause, Kuyper and the orthodox party employed journalism, education, and even political action. Two newspapers, *The Standard,* a daily publication, and *The Herald,* a weekly edition, vigorously promoted orthodoxy while calling readers to lives of Christ-likeness and devotion to duty as the Lord's people. These organs were champions of parents' right to provide the education they desired for their children, as they regarded schools as part of the domain Christ claims for himself. On the masthead of *The Herald* was the motto *For a Free Church in a Free Land.* Years of struggle and many defeats on the way did not deter this endeavor.

Because only the national legislature could end the state monopoly over education, Kuyper led the way in forming the Anti-Revolutionary Party, a Christian political movement to assert Christ's cause in public life. By then Kuyper had become pastor of the *Nieuwkerk* in Amsterdam, a city known as a center of liberalism. His fervent preaching and staunch orthodoxy drew large crowds, nevertheless, as he continued in his role as defender of the faith and, as a consequence, faced hostility from officials of the National Synod and their supporters in church and state. Kuyper strove to dissolve the National Synod in order to restore lost autonomy to local congregations, for he believed that was essential for the success of genuine reformation. All through this struggle, Kuyper urged his people to engage in zealous evangelism.

Since he regarded Christian education as indispensable for the success of his projects, Abraham Kuyper in 1874 left his pastoral position to seek a seat in parliament, where he could promote legislation to free Christian families from the burden of taxation to fund public schools. Only education in truth could combat the prevailing humanism, so he sought tax relief and government payments to private schools as chosen by parents. In this endeavor especially he was the champion of the *kleine luyden* (common people) who, until then, had no right to vote and, therefore, little influence in affairs of state. When Kuyper won a seat in parliament, he led efforts to enlarge the electorate, and by 1896 49% of adult males could vote, whereas that figure had been only 12% in

[9] An account of these events appears in James Edward McGoldrick, *God's Renaissance Man: the Life and work of Abraham Kuyper* (Darlington, England: Evangelical Press, 2000), 20-45.

1870.[10] The Anti-Revolutionary Party did not seek a theocracy (or "ecclesiocracy") but a separation of church and state into distinct, but not alien, spheres of authority. Always the party respected the rights of non-Christians. Kuyper knew the Netherlands had become a diverse society, and he sought the same freedom in education for secular humanists and Roman Catholics that he desired for his own Reformed Protestants. A Roman Catholic political party soon formed in response to the Anti-Revolutionary Party, and the two movements shared a common interest in freedom for their schools. Collaboration between them in 1889 led to partial success, when Parliament enacted a law to grant private schools one-third of their expenses from public funds. Full funding did not occur until 1917, but the state monopoly over education ended in 1889.

Concurrent with the effort to obtain equality for private schools there was a comparable movement in higher education. The initial success in this regard came with the creation of the Free University of Amsterdam. Kuyper began advocating freedom for private universities in 1875, when he asked parliament for such recognition. In the face of opposition from the three public universities, he organized the Association for Higher Education on Reformed Principles, which gained the status of a legal corporation in 1879. Creation of a Christian university became a matter of some urgency when the Dutch Universities Act (1877) removed the teaching of theology from the university curriculum and replaced it with comparative religion. Thereafter all public institutions were to be neutral toward all religions, including Christianity. Kuyper reasoned that formation of a theological seminary would be an inadequate response to this legislation, so he proposed a full-orbed university committed to the Reformed faith. He desired not only sound instruction in theology, but an entire curriculum based on a biblical worldview. The Netherlands then needed a school in which all professors would be informed believers who would teach all disciplines from a Christian point of view.[11] At first the state required graduates of the Free University to pass qualifying examinations at one of its universities to validate their degrees, and the Dutch Reformed Church refused to ordain graduates of the Christian university as ministers.

During his tenure as a professor at the Free University (1880-

[10]   Bernard Vlekke, *Evolution of the Dutch Nation* (New York: Roy Publishers, 1945), 316-21.
[11]   See McGoldrick, *God's Renaissance Man*, 52-61 and Wilhelm Kolfhaus, "The Significance of Abraham Kuyper for Reformed Theology," *Evangelical Quarterly 2* (1930): 302-12.

1901), Abraham Kuyper eventually convinced the civil authorities to recognize degrees from the university he founded, and in 1901, he became Prime Minister of the Netherlands at the head of a coalition government formed in collaboration with the Catholic Party. In that position he obtained legislation which granted equality to private universities and other schools. The Free University was still the only private institution of its kind, but in 1923 the Roman Catholics opened the University of Nijmegen under the provisions of the law Kuyper had introduced in 1903.

Consistent with his worldview, Kuyper argued for a university with a confessional basis where instruction proceeds on subscription to objective truth. He allowed for pluralism in education rather than to deprive secularists of their rights and showed himself thereby to be more tolerant than the liberals who had tried to preserve the state monopoly. He, of course, rejected the humanists' claim to neutrality in learning, because he knew all pursuits of knowledge begin with assumptions of faith that cannot be verified empirically. Christians begin with a commitment to the sovereignty of God; secularists assume the autonomy of man. Both are dogmatists.

Abraham Kuyper and the Anti-Revolutionary Party sought justice in all areas of life but concentrated on freedom for Christian schools, humane policy in the Dutch colonies, and protection for industrial workers often subject to exploitation. Kuyper did not want the church to become a political or educational institution, so he did not establish church schools or a church newspaper. He sought parent-controlled schools and a university separate from the church as well as the state. The Anti-Revolutionary Party was not a clerical organization but one which functioned with Christian principles in the political sphere. Through his party and his service in parliament, Kuyper led his beloved *common people* out of political isolation to become involved in public life, there to affirm the rights of Christ in society at large, not only in the church.

FACING THE ANTITHESIS

First as a Member of Parliament, later as Prime Minister, Abraham Kuyper opposed both liberals and conservatives because those parties espoused a humanist worldview. He adamantly opposed the various socialist factions because of their overt materialism and their inclination toward violence to gain their objectives. In his opinion, the conflicts between the Anti-Revolutionary Party and its secular opponents were due not only to incompatible material aspirations. They, on the contrary, reflected the collision of irreconcilable life-principles. For him the manner in which people regard God, themselves, and the universe stands as the crux of the battle between good and evil, a struggle in which the opposing forces have no common ground. The current term *culture war* would have served Kuyper well. In this engagement it will not do to reply to the enemies' attacks in a piecemeal manner when two antithetical worldviews are locked in mortal combat. "Principle must be arrayed against principle," since a clash of life systems is in progress.[12] Only Calvinism has the means to wage this struggle effectively.

Kuyper supported his concept of antithesis by citing the battle cry of the French Revolution, *No God, No Master,* as evidence that secularists aim to "free" mankind from divine authority. The Reformed faith alone provides a comprehensive system embracing man's relation to God, to other men, and to the world. Calvinism can do this because it does not restrict itself to ecclesiastical and theological matters.[13] It emphasizes both the dignity of man as God's image-bearer and his depravity as a sinner in rebellion against divine authority. In Kuyper's own words, "every man, simply because he is a man, should be recognized, respected, and dealt with as a creature created after the divine likeness."[14]

Calvinism, in contrast to the idea of equality popular in the French Revolution, desires to see all humans "on their knees before God, consumed with a common zeal for the glory of his name."[15] The only social distinctives Calvinism recognizes are those God has mandated by conferring his gifts and the authority that pertains to offices that people occupy in his providence.

Although God created human beings with the dignity of his own image, the fall has corrupted human nature in all its facets, and that includes the mind, blinded by sin to its own condition. Apart from the regenerating power of the Holy Spirit, a fallen human "does not perceive and cannot perceive, the real condition of his own being, nor of his reason."[16] This renders futile efforts to prove God to unregenerate people. That would be like displaying a beautiful jewel before a blind

---

[12]   Abraham Kuyper, *Lectures on Calvinism* (Grand Rapids: William B. Eerdmans Publishing Company, 1931), 11-12.
[13]   Ibid., 19-23.
[14]   Ibid., 27.
[15]   Ibid., 28.
[16]   Kuyper, *Principles of Sacred Theology,* 384-85.

person and expecting him to appreciate it. Likewise, secularists assume the world is in its natural condition because they maintain a worldview that excludes God, so Christians must challenge their basic principles and ask the Holy Spirit to remove their blindness and to make the claims of Scripture convincing. It is a great mercy that God has not left humans to depend upon their depraved reason but has sent his Spirit to regenerate them, thereby to convince and enable them to accept the truth of revelation.[17] "Were the Holy Scriptures," wrote Kuyper, "to be carried into the world without the regenerating and illumining activity of the Holy Spirit to precede, accompany, and to follow it, no church would ever be seen among the nations."[18]

In assessing the significance of human depravity and the consequent antithesis it has produced between regenerate and unregenerate minds, Kuyper declared:

> we are not dealing with isolated sinful facts but a power of sin that controls sinful life in all its expressions. All sin has a common face, bears the stamp of a common origin, shows a well-ordered coherence in its manifestations and a regular development in its progress. In a word, there is a *history* of sin....Sin puts the stamp of God's image on its own counterfeit currency and misuses its God-given powers to imitate God's authority....Sin lives solely by plagiarizing the ideas of God.[19]

Kuyper's perception of the human condition led him to reject a rationalistic method of apologetics. He believed unregenerate people do not have the capacity to be objective in assessing the claims of God. Kuyper therefore called Christians to attack the *basis* of anti-Christian worldviews, and he believed the very meaning of life is at stake in this contest. Sin has disposed the mind against God, so it does not operate properly and cannot be neutral toward its Creator. A person's worldview reflects the moral and spiritual condition of one's mind. A worldview then is not an abstract idea but a genuine expression of one's moral state.[20]

---

[17]   Ibid., 387-402; 557-61.

[18]   Ibid., 634.

[19]   Kuyper; "Uniformity: the Curse of Modern Life," in *Centennial Reader,* 21-23.

[20]   A perceptive analysis of Kuyper's contribution on this point and on the whole matter of the mind appears in David Naugle, *Worldview: the History of a Concept* (Grand

The insistence that the defense of Christianity must feature a systematic assertion of principles rather than a rebuttal of specific arguments is a conviction Kuyper developed after reading a work of James Orr (1844-1913), a Scottish Presbyterian theologian and historian. In 1891, Orr delivered lectures later published as *The Christian View of God and the World.* In this impressive book of great erudition, the author maintained Christians must respond to competing worldviews with comprehensive statements of their position, for nothing less could be effective.[21]

Agreeing with Orr, Kuyper affirmed the lordship of Christ over all creation, a truth he presented forcefully in his own *Lectures on Calvinism* in 1898. There he cited modernism/secularism as the arch-enemy of God's truth, especially modernism as expressed in the ideas that undergirded the French Revolution, Darwinian evolution, and German pantheism. Kuyper contended that traditional defenses of particular doctrines could not avail in this struggle. Only the full-orbed worldview, which Calvinism alone can produce, could be effective.[22] He knew learned modernists presented their views in logical, coherent arguments based on their axiomatic principles, so Christians must do nothing less. In his lecture "Calvinism and the Future," he declared: "against this deadly danger [modernism] you cannot successfully defend your sanctuary but by placing in opposition to all this, a *life-and-world view of your own, founded as firmly on the base of your own principles, wrought out with the same clearness and glittering in an equally logical consistency.*"[23]

To illustrate the need for a systematic defense, Abraham Kuyper cited conflicts between Christians and secularists in science. Such controversies are not due to the relative quality of scholarship as one camp engages the other. Instead they are results of opposing assumptions about the present state of the universe. Modernists hold the world as it is now is in a normal condition and develops through natural evolution. Christians, however, maintain that the present condition is abnormal because of the cosmic effects of sin and that only divine action can

---

Rapids: William B. Eerdmans Publishing Company, 2002), 256 ff.
    [21]   Ibid., 7-14; James Orr, *The Christian View of God and the World* (NewYork: Anson D. F. Randolph and Company, 1893); especially lecture III.
    [22]   Kuyper, *Lectures on Calvinism,* 135-36; for a keen analysis of Kuyper's *Lectures,* see Peter S. Heslam, *Creating a Christian Worldview* (Grand Rapids: William B. Eerdmans Publishing Company, 1998).
    [23]   Kuyper, *Lectures on Calvinism,* 190.

restore it to its original state.[24] Cosmic redemption is then the major feature of the Christian worldview.

Whether a person accepts the modernist-secularist hypothesis or the opposing Christian belief will be a consequence of his or her religious and philosophical axioms. There is no actual conflict between faith and science, and every scientific investigation begins with an act of faith. All scientists assume their sense perceptions are accurate and their logic correct. The perceived conflict is due to mutually exclusive assumptions about the condition of the universe, which neither camp can verify empirically. Each position has its own Supreme Being "as the point of departure for [its] worldview, and "those starting points are mutually exclusive since, for the secularist man is ultimate, but for the Christian God is supreme."[25] Spiritual regeneration or the lack thereof determines where people stand with regard to the claims of God. "He who is not born again," Kuyper contended, "cannot have a substantial knowledge *of* sin and he who is not converted cannot possess certainty of faith; he who lacks the *testimonium Spiritus Sancti* cannot believe the Holy Scriptures."[26]

COMMON GRACE

Although Abraham Kuyper was emphatic about the noetic and cosmic effects of sin and the depravity of fallen nature, he understood that humans can accomplish relative good despite their unregenerate condition. Such attainments he attributed to the operations of common grace, which "does not kill the core of sin, nor. . . save unto eternal life, but it arrests the complete effectuation of sin, just as human insight arrests the fury of wild beasts. . . . In a similar manner God, by his *common grace,* restrains the operation of sin in man partly by breaking its power, partly by taming his evil spirit, and partly by domesticating his nation or his family."[27]

Since humans are sinners in rebellion against God, He owes them no favors whatever, but in his kindness he has granted various gifts to the rebels and thereby makes possible a relatively stable and enjoyable life on earth. God has not abandoned his creation but rather intends to restore it to its former glory. Common grace is the means of preservation,

---

[24]   Ibid., 130-31.
[25]   Ibid., 133.
[26]   Ibid., 137.
[27]   Ibid., 123-24.

a prelude to full restoration. The Holy Spirit makes the work of common grace effective, as he guides history toward its goal. Along the way he bestows talents and abilities upon both regenerate and unregenerate people so that even the latter make valuable contributions in the nature of civic good. The historic documents of the Reformed faith affirm this teaching, for example, the *Canons of Dort*, III, iv, 4 and the *Belgic Confession.*[28]

As people enjoy the benefits of common grace, they are responsible to be good stewards of creation. The creation mandate (Gen. 1:27-31) requires this, but sin has made them ungrateful and irresponsible. Regeneration changes that attitude radically, so that Christians operate in the arena of common grace as servants of God and man, and they respect nature as a gift of grace. Through science, technology, government service, and private enterprise they have the means to maintain their proper relationship to creation.[29]   Although common grace brings benefits to everyone, the elect benefit most, because it creates conditions in which they hear the gospel and come to Christ. Jesus is not, however, only the redeemer of the elect, but the reconciler of the creation to God and the re-creator of the heavens and the earth. One day the whole world will "be his conquest, the trophy of his glory."[30]

While unbelievers will not honor God as the source of their talents, Christians must do exactly that. In the course of their grateful employment of God's gifts, they must be *Christian* in all their pursuits. They must reject any sacred-secular dichotomy and remember every inch of creation belongs to their Savior. Christ has not abandoned the world, so neither may his people. Since God works by both *special* and *common* grace, Christians are not to leave such areas as art, science, technology, and politics to unbelievers. Affirming the kingship of Christ negates a world-denying pietism that assigns priority to protecting oneself from the evils of society. Although the world is in a corrupted condition, it is not under the rule of Satan, evil humans, or impersonal fate. Christ is king, now and forever![31] "There is no doubt," argued Kuyper, "...that common grace and special grace come most intimately connected from their

---

[28]   Vincent E. Bacote, *The Spirit in Public Theology* (Grand Rapids: Baker Academic Books, 2005), 127.
[29]   Ibid., 144; Kuyper, "Common Grace," in *Centennial Reader*, 167-71.
[30]   Kuyper, "Common Grace," in *Centennial Reader*, 171.
[31]   Ibid., 166.

origin, and this connection lies in Christ."[32] His church then must do two things: it nourishes the souls of the elect, and by its indirect influence, constrains the non-elect as well to acts of civic virtue.[33]

Although the church is an influence for good in society at large, it must not attempt to impose its confession upon the state. It should instead exert moral authority without seeking authoritarian control over society. The city of God and the city of this world are separate; light from the city of God illumines the other city, as believers fulfill their duty to be "the light of the world" (Matt. 5:14).[34]

In an 1891 address to a convention of the Anti-Revolutionary Party, Abraham Kuyper forcefully decried Christians who deny or ignore Christ's authority in politics, and he assailed that attitude as capitulation to evil. Kuyper blamed the French Revolution for spreading humanist ideas contrary to divine revelation, and he concluded that humanism had brought the worship of man and had made earth, not heaven, the final point of reference. He accused religious humanists of perverting the church as a way to subvert the Christian faith, and public schools he identified as the primary instruments to further the humanists' agenda. Kuyper was especially pointed in his critique of public universities in which Darwinian professors taught students to regard themselves as animals rather than bearers of God's image.[35]

Kuyper's opposition to Darwinism was in part because it leads to the belief that material prosperity is the ultimate good. This view and the state policy that promotes it will cause morality to "degenerate into the pursuit of utility until, in the end, even though people do not descend from the animal world, [it] will degrade them into brutes."[36]

Speaking for the community of Reformed believers, Kuyper said, "Calvinists...thank God for making it possible for men to dwell together in a well-ordered society and for restraining us personally from horrible sins." For this reason, rather than leave the arts and sciences to unbelievers, Calvinists seek to explore all God's works, and they do so within the respective spheres of activity which God has ordained, for they insist every inch of creation belongs to Christ.[37]

---

[32]   Ibid., 187. Kuyper supported this assertion with a reference to Col. 1:15-18.
[33]   Ibid., 190.
[34]   Ibid., 200.
[35]   Ibid., 208-12.
[36]   Ibid., 224.
[37]   Kuyper, *Lectures on Calvinism,* 125-28.

CONCLUSION

Abraham Kuyper, it is obvious, was not a mere theorist, but one who sought specific means by which to implement his worldview. The Anti-Revolutionary Party, the Free University of Amsterdam, and his newspapers, all illustrate his activism. While he regarded Christians as pilgrims on the way to heaven, he called them to accept responsibility to perform their duties on earth, which includes exploring the resources of creation while working with them to glorify the Creator. In doing so Christians must remember the antithesis between themselves and unregenerate people who consider the condition of the world as normal![38] In the sphere of education this recognition is of crucial importance, so believers must not be content to pursue theology while leaving the other academic disciplines to non-Christians. To do that is to employ "the tactics of the ostrich," and thereby to ignore Christ's claim to every inch.[39] "Wherever man may stand," argued Kuyper, "whatever he may do,...in agriculture, in commerce, and in industry, or his mind, in the world of art, and science, he is...constantly standing before the face of his God,...he has strictly to obey his God, and above all, he has to aim at the glory of his God."[40]

Kuyper, of course, knew the present sinful state of humanity causes even regenerate people to misunderstand their proper relationship to the various spheres of life. There is always a temptation to regard the practice of one's faith as an emotional experience and an escape from the problems of earthly existence. Consistently pursued, this leads to ignoring public life as though it were unrelated to faith. True Christianity, however, is not confined to feelings, since "God has ordained...laws...for all of life,...the Calvinist demands that all of life be consecrated to his service."[41]

The overriding principle of Calvinism is *cosmological,* that is, the affirmation of divine sovereignty over all of creation, so "the Calvinist will not shut himself in his church and abandon the world to its

---

[38]   Ibid., 130-32.
[39]   Ibid., 139.
[40]   Ibid., 53.
[41]   Ibid.

fate."[42] He will, to the contrary, proclaim a worldview that addresses the fundamental issues most pertinent to human needs. This will necessarily produce a conflict between Christians and the secular culture around them, as regenerate and unregenerate minds interpret reality differently. The diversity of world views is due to the noetic effects of sin and to the activity of evil forces, since "our struggle is not against flesh and blood, but against. . . the powers of this dark world and against spiritual forces of evil in the heavenly realms" (Eph. 6:12, NIV). Since God has intervened into history from the outside, his revelation makes it possible to have an accurate worldview. He has already revealed the meaning of creation, so humans are not free to assign their own meanings to it. Creatures must not try to supplant their Creator, which is exactly what rigorous humanists seek to do. God's law is the standard of judgment, so moral values are not mere sentiments or conventions. The biblical worldview presents "an absolutist perspective on life that is real, true, and good."[43] Humans form their worldviews in terms of their acceptance of God or as a consequence of their idolatry. Those who presume they are autonomous engage in rebellion against God, and such people cannot understand the world or themselves correctly. They participate in the war of good against evil on the side of evil, contesting Christ's claim to every inch of the *cosmos.*[44]

Worldviews are important because they show how people and societies perceive reality, and they affect how people answer the deepest questions of life and its significance.[45] Modern secularists deny the reality of sin and so blame social structures and institutions for the unhappiness and misery humans must endure. Rather than admit the need for regeneration, they justify revolution as the means to change such structures. As Kuyper expressed this matter, humanists fail to "comprehend the true context, the proper coherence, and the systematic unity of all things."[46] Because of the noetic effects of sin, unbelievers do not see the connection of creatures to their Creator. Like animals that see objects but do not understand their structure or purpose, unregenerate minds do not see created beings and objects as parts of God's panorama.

---

[42]   Ibid., 73.
[43]   Naugle, *Worldview,* 266. Chapter nine of this work is an insightful analysis, one on which I have drawn extensively.
[44]   Ibid., 275-83.
[45]   Ibid., 345.
[46]   Kuyper, "Common Grace," 449.

They view the universe without appreciation for its Architect.[47] The antithesis between *natural* and *spiritual* man (I Cor. 2: 11-15) does not stop with their conflicting assessments of either general or special revelation. It extends to all of life, as only recipients of regenerating grace achieve "a view of the world that is in harmony with the truth and the essence of things."[48]

Abraham Kuyper knew the development of social structures through common grace would not produce perfection, something that would occur only at the return of Christ. He was a *Neocalvinist* in that he adapted the principles of the Reformed faith to the needs of his own era because he believed improving the human condition is a Christian responsibility. He never promoted social-cultural development as his ultimate concern; for he understood mankind's greatest need is forgiveness for its sins to be obtained only through faith in Christ. While he rejoiced that common grace enables even unbelievers to make useful contributions, Kuyper remembered their sinful refusal to glorify God for his gifts. He therefore urged Christians to seek the salvation of the lost, that they too would acclaim Christ's dominion over every inch.

[47]   Ibid., 450.
[48]   Ibid., 458.

Chapter 3

Islam, *Hamas* and Peculiar Providence[1]

George Grant

In the book of Habakkuk we read:

The oracle that Habakkuk the prophet saw.

O LORD, how long shall I cry for help, and you will not hear? Or cry to you "Violence!" and you will not save? Why do you make me see iniquity, and why do you idly look at wrong. Destruction and violence are before me; strife and contention arise. So the law is paralyzed, and justice never goes forth. For the wicked surround the righteous; so justice goes forth perverted. Look among the nations, and see; wonder and be astounded. For I am doing a work in your days that you would not believe if told. For behold, I am raising up the Chaldeans, that bitter and hasty nation, who march through the breadth of the earth, to seize dwellings not their own. They are dreaded and fearsome; their justice and dignity go forth from themselves. Their horses are swifter than leopards, more fierce than the evening wolves; their horsemen press proudly on. Their horsemen come from afar; they fly like an eagle swift to devour. They all come for violence, all their faces forward. They gather captives like sand. At kings they scoff, and at rulers they laugh. They laugh at every fortress, for they pile up earth and take it. Then

[1]   George Grant PhD is Senior Pastor of Parish Presbyterian Church (PCA) in Franklin, Tennessee and Director of King's Meadow Study Center. This is an edited transcription of an address delivered at the Spring Theology Conference of Greenville Presbyterian Theological Seminary on March 13, 2007.

they sweep by like the wind and go on, guilty men, whose own might is their god!

Are you not from everlasting, O LORD my God, my Holy One? We shall not die. O LORD, you have ordained them as a judgment, and you, O Rock, have established them for reproof. You who are of purer eyes than to see evil and cannot look at wrong, why do you idly look at traitors   and are silent when the wicked swallows up the man more righteous than he? You make mankind like the fish of the sea, like crawling things that have no ruler. He brings all of them up with a hook; he drags them out with his net; he gathers them in his dragnet; so he rejoices and is glad. Therefore he sacrifices to his net and makes offerings to his dragnet; for by them he lives in luxury, and his food is rich. Is he then to keep on emptying his net and mercilessly killing nations forever?[2]

Thus says the Word of the Lord.

We live in troubled times and, it is not an overstatement to say, we are a troubled people. We see men, bitter and hasty nations, like the Chaldeans of Habakkuk's time, marching the breadth of the earth to seize buildings not their own to bring dread and fearsomeness into the conversations of men and women and children the world over. And we, the covenant people of God, oft times wonder, "Where is your justice, Lord, in days like these?"

In March 2007 the 43rd generation direct descendant of Mohammed the prophet made a state visit to the United States and addressed a joint session of the House and the Senate in the United States Capital in Washington DC. He came to make a plea for peace, this heir of the Hashemite dynasty, a long time caretaker through all of the Caliphates and all of the dynasties of the ancient Islamic world, the caretakers of all of the holy places of Mecca and Medina. He came before the United States House and Senate to ask the United States to exercise its considerable wealth and manpower to bring peace to the world by settling the divide between Israelis and Palestinians.

The man before our legislative leaders was King Abdullah II of Jordan, educated in the United States at the Deerfield Academy, and later at Oxford University and Sandhurst. He is very articulate and his soaring oratory and high-minded rhetoric demanded the respect of every

---

[2]   Hab 1:1-17. Unless otherwise noted all Scripture quotations are taken from the *English Standard Version*, 2001.

congressman and every Senator, every general and every bureaucrat in the room.

I was privileged to be there at the invitation of the administration and I sat in the visitor's gallery surrounded by a sea of $2000 Armani suits and $800 Gucci shoes. I felt like a shabby Presbyterian preacher for sure. But as I listened to this high sounding oratory, this heart-felt plea for the United States once again to weigh in to the conflict that seems to spark so many other conflicts around the world, my mind was drawn immediately to the book of Habakkuk and particularly the first chapter of Habakkuk.

Now, I'm not the first reformed type to make associations between the world of Islam and the problems that it brings and its conflict with the West and the book of Habakkuk. The great reformed thinker and mentor to John Calvin, Martin Bucer, spent six months preaching through the book of Habakkuk at his little congregation in the city of Strasbourg and made the connection in the 16th century, a time when Islam was rattling sabers and marching on the West gobbling up huge portions of the Balkans and ultimately, in Bucer's lifetime, arriving within 50 miles of Vienna with its massive armies and threats of bringing Dar al Islam to the place where it would cover the whole of the populated earth.

Bucer said that in order to understand the worldview of Islam we must first come to grips with the message of Habakkuk. Habakkuk the prophet is an interesting fellow. We don't know much about this, the eighth of the 12 Minor Prophets. We don't know his father's name. We don't know his hometown. We don't know of his tribe. He is a bit of an enigma in that much of his prophecy—abbreviated as it is in three short chapters—is comprised of a series of complaints followed by a worldview seminar of sorts, a worship service, and a Shigionoth, a hymn of praise to a God of providence and purpose.

Jeremiah, his contemporary, was known as the weeping prophet for his bitter lamentations. Nahum was known as the woeful prophet for his baleful predictions. According to Charles Haddon Spurgeon, Habakkuk is the flustered prophet. And he was, indeed, flustered. He was frustrated with Judah. He was frustrated with the king. He was frustrated with God. In fact, as we peruse his complaints we discover that Habakkuk was frustrated with just about everyone except himself.
He lived at the end of the seventh century BC and the beginning of the sixth century. It was a difficult time in the land of Israel. Josiah's great reforms are now a distant memory. Jehoiakim is now a king, but he is

intent on the very path from which his father had so powerfully arrested and wrenched the nation. He was a wicked and a perverse man as we read in 2 Kings 23 and 2 Chronicles 34 and the chapters that follow—the long story that chronicles the epoch from Josiah to Zedekiah and the fall of Judah. These were sad and sorry days, indeed, for the nation of Judah. Jeremiah the prophet talks about the wickedness in Jeremiah chapters 22 through 26 and because of all of this wickedness, Habakkuk is frustrated. There is an interesting little notation in chapter one, verse one, that indicates that Habakkuk was somehow an official prophet, perhaps a court prophet. This is not a biblically-ordained institution, but apparently there are a number of indications that after Josiah's reforms, in order to ensure that never again would the covenant people of God forget their covenant privileges and forget their covenant responsibilities, a prophet was assigned the official role of announcing to the peoples their call to obedience.

It is possible that Habakkuk held this official role. It would have been a role as an ambassador pressing the claims of God's sovereignty, prosecuting covenantal lawsuits and calling the people to repentance. Thus, in verse one we are told that this prophet, *the prophet*, was given a message-burden—literally a message that was an oracle and a burden simultaneously. The message was simple. The people of God have run after wickedness, debauchery, concupiscence and lasciviousness. (Don't you just love those King James words?)

With great fervor Jeremiah describes it in Jeremiah 22:17, "But you have eyes and heart only for your dishonest gain, for shedding innocent blood, and for practicing oppression and violence." The land was filled with wickedness. In fact, according to Habakkuk the land had become a theater of violence.

You notice how many times, in the first three verses, Habakkuk uses that word "violence?" It is the Hebrew word *hamas*. It isn't any old garden variety of violence. *Hamas* means senseless, cruel, mad violence. It's the violence of a terrorist bombing. It is the violence of a drive-by-shooting. It is the violence of a carjacking. It is the violence of child abuse. It is senseless, mindless violence. It is the violence of sensationalistic Hollywood.

Hamas. The land was full of this *hamas* according to verse three, full of iniquity and strife and contention. In fact, law and order had broken down and the wicked prevailed and justice was perverted (v. 4) and so Habakkuk, the official court prophet, cries out "O LORD, how long shall I cry for help?" (v. 2) "Why must I see this?" (v. 3)

In verse five God answers Habakkuk's covenantal complaint and allows to Habakkuk that this answer is going to be a bit unexpected. God says, I am about to do something astounding. This action of mine is imminent. I am raising up, he says, the Babylonians, the Chaldeans, a bitter, hasty, barbaric people, a horrible, a dreaded and fearsome nation. And they will, according to verses six and seven, Come and plunder the land. They are faster and more powerful than anything you will have ever seen Habakkuk, (v. 8). In fact, they are a law unto themselves and their might is their god,(vv. 10 and 11). Indeed, their dignity goes forth from themselves, (v. 7).

In a sense what God does is to come to the prophet and the prophet cries out, as it were, "Lord, the land is full of *hamas, hamas,* senseless, terrible, mindless, cruel violence." God says, "You think you know *hamas?* I'll show you *hamas.* Israel likes *hamas?* The kingdom of Judah wants to revel in *hamas?* Fine. I'll give you *hamas* in spades." Habakkuk, of course, is stunned in silence. He begins back pedaling almost immediately. He straightens his prophet's mantle and he begins to rehearse and recite his catechism. Did you notice that beginning at verse 12? "But, Lord. I know you're...this is probably hyperbole, right, Lord? Because I know you, God. I know that you are everlasting, you are personal, you are holy, you are the sovereign judge. You are our rock, the rock of our salvation. You are our refuge. You are our fortress. You are our deliverer, right, God?" (v. 13) "Lord, you have pure eyes, too pure to look upon evil. I know you, Lord. I know all about you and I've got the verses to prove it. And, Lord, what you are proposing is not consistent with your character. What you are proposing is not consistent with your attributes."

God's answer to Habakkuk did not match his preconceived ideas about who and what God was, what God would do. It didn't match up. So he begins to school God in the attributes of God. Of this passage Martin Bucer once said, "Theology's greatest dangers come when we attempt to squeeze our doctrines and experience into the mold of our prejudices."[3]

The problem to Habakkuk, you see, was that mankind seems to be reduced to a mere swarming. The Babylonians are then made the fishers of men, verses 14 through 17. And God, above all else, has somehow, some way, forgotten the scale of righteousness with the result

---

[3]   Cited in W. Garden Blaikie, *Chalmers and the Ten Years Conflict: A History of the Disruption* (Edinburgh: Oliphant and Anderson, 1891), 116.

being that he is allowing wicked men to swallow up others more righteous than they.

Now, we can see Habakkuk's errors so clearly precisely because they are the very errors that we make over and over and over again. Notice them very quickly. First of all, Habakkuk has this very narrow view of providence. It's likely that this narrow view of providence is the result of the fact that Habakkuk is a failed prophet. It was his responsibility to be the watchman on the wall and the nation, instead of prospering under his watch, was in no great shakes. The result is that he is frustrated and flustered and now he wants God to come and bail him out. His pride is wounded as an unsuccessful prophet and now he wants backup and God is not giving to him like he thought that he ought. So the prophet has this very narrow of view of God's providence—what is possible, what is probable, what God does and does not want at any particular time in history. And he baptizes his own prejudices upon that narrow view of providence and he demands that God operate outside of his predetermined box. As J.B. Phillips said so long ago, "Habakkuk's God is just too small."

Secondly, Habakkuk has God all figured out. Habakkuk's God is tame and predictable. He operates according to formulas. Therefore, Habakkuk is outraged when things don't go according to plan. You see, for Habakkuk God's righteousness and his justice are all according to scale, Habakkuk's scale and, therefore, Habakkuk is flustered and angry. D. Martyn Lloyd-Jones once said, "However precise we may be in our theological formulations, when we attempt to define our world and God's actions in the world according to our own predilections we go the way of the Babylonians, all together missing the import of the gospel."[4]

Third, Habakkuk wants righteousness and wickedness to be measured to scale, in terms of human achievement. Habakkuk seems to misapply "Do this and live," making it a theology that the doctrines of grace so adamantly stand against. Habakkuk wants more wicked people to be measured against slightly less wicked people and for God to judge in favor of the slightly less wicked people, to favor them, to bless them, and then to whip them into shape and clean them up afterwards. Alas, we do the same thing again and again and again. It's a peculiar form of works righteousness that we fit into our doctrine of sanctification if not our doctrine of justification.

---

[4]   Martyn Lloyd-Jones, *Christ our Freedom* (Cambridge: InterVarsity Fellowship, 1939), 3.

Fourth, therefore, Habakkuk really was revealed in chapter one as a true heir of the Babylonians rather than as an heir of Abraham, Isaac and Jacob. He has a Babylonish heart and God is showing him his Babylonish heart by bringing the Babylonians like a swarm upon the land.

I take special delight in really bright students. I love students who have all the answers. They are quick to get their hands up in the air when I ask a question. They are the ones in the back who—or perhaps in the front—who are always going, "Ooh, ooh, ooh, ooh, ooh, ooh, ooh, ooh," before I even get the question out of my mouth. I love those students. They are sharp. They are provocative. But the one thing that I have discovered all through the years is that there is a distinct disadvantage to having every answer down pat.

Augustine once said, "Measure me by my worst student, please."[5] There is great wisdom in that. After all, the essence of the gospel, the chief mark of a life of grace, is repentance. It's not necessarily having all of the answers down pat. After all, our righteousness is as filthy garments the prophet says. Not our wickedness, not our also ran efforts, our righteousness is as filthy garments. It is our competency often times that gets us into the deepest trouble. It is when we know the answers and we are certain about the course of action and we have got God nailed. That's when our hubris makes its ugly appearance. You know what hubris is, right? Pride on steroids. At any rate the fact is that when we know all of the answers, when we have got it all figured out, when we can define God on a single sheet of paper, when we can plot his actions on a flow chart, that is when we are in trouble.

What emerges out of a worldview like that, a systemic, structural, mechanical, ideological perspective of the world and the God who created the world, the kind of worldview that produces is necessarily a worldview of violence. It is the worldview of *hamas*. Now, that may seem like a long way around the block for you to get to Islam, but the chief marks of Islam are not the five pillars. The chief marks of Islam are not the incidental aspects of jihad or the *zakat* tax or the *salat* prayer. No, all of those things are second and third order consequences of an ideological system.

You must understand, Mohammed the prophet had a very narrow view of providence. He knew what God could, would, and should do.

---

[5]   Cited in Blaikie, *Chalmers and the Ten Years Conflict*, 121.

He defined it carefully. He established its parameters. He drew up its profile in a series of discourses that were iron clad, so easy to understand that any peasant from Mecca or Medina or, for that matter, any intellectual or congressman could actually understand it. It's a system that does not need repentance. It is a system that does not need to have a theology of the fall because it is so mechanically systemic and ideologically iron clad that all you have to do is follow the rules, check the boxes, go through the steps, keep the fasts, make the pilgrimage and all is well. Except that all is not well.

Mark Twain once said, "You can't depend upon your eyes when your imagination is out of focus." We might paraphrase that by saying, "You can't depend upon your theology when your heart is out of focus." It seems a little backwards, doesn't it? You can't depend upon your theology when your heart is out of focus, but the fact is that virtually every heresy that the world has ever seen has sprung originally out of an embedded sin pattern that had to be justified, that had to be reconciled somehow with faith. Therefore, an ideological system was constructed, built around this sin pattern, this predilection to wickedness so that the wickedness itself could be justified.

That's the essence of Islam, which is exactly the essence of Mormonism, which is why the two look so much alike. When you peel back all of the layers of the peculiar methods of meditation and search for peace and harmony and serendipity and all of the activities of global and local peace that is the heart and soul of Zen Buddhism, the save-the-starving-third-world-lesbian-codependent-whales crowd, the essence of it is the same again, the same bottom line. So, in the first place the worldview of Islam is buttressed by a narrow view of God's providence. Here is what God can do and here is what God cannot do according to our system. That means that in these ideological systems God is all figured out. He is tame and predictable even when—as in Islam—God is remote and fierce; his fierceness is like that of Zeus—capricious, but predictable. As a result, and a second point, Islam really has no ability to take into account man because man is neither created in the image of Allah, nor is man a fallen being; therefore, there can be no basis for a systemic sociology which is why people in Islam don't ultimately matter in this life. It's why in Islamic countries regardless of socioeconomic status we find the lowest literacy rates, the highest infant mortality rates in the world; because people don't matter.

Third, Islam is predicated on a works righteousness system. Therefore, everything is built around a scale of righteousness. I had an

Imam once tell me that in essence the doctrine of Islamic holiness is akin to the old joke about the two men being chased by a bear. One of whom was not at all frightened. His friend said, "Why are you not frightened? He says, "I'm faster than you." You only have to be a little faster than the next guy, only slightly more righteous. In a scale-of-righteousness system where God grades on the curve, like in Mrs. Guidry's geometry class, all you have to do is figure out the system, work the system, work the angles. Therefore, it is not surprising that these kinds of ideologies produce conniving, manipulative, deceptive kinds of cultures. They are the heirs of the Babylonians. And the end result is that *hamas* marks their relations.

As Martin Luther said about this passage, "A man frustrated with the darkness of error, unable to come to the truth, must necessarily resolve himself in either violence or despair, the only two alternatives left."[6]

As I sat in the gallery of the United States Senate and listened to King Abdullah speak about the need for peace I kept thinking of *hamas*. I kept thinking of Hezbollah. I kept thinking of Al Quaida. All the soaring rhetoric and all the high-minded oratory in the world cannot remove the taint of a worldview that is marked by a narrow view of providence where God is all figured out or where men are judged on a scale of righteousness and where, in their hearts, they are but the heirs of the Babylonians.

With a culture like that you can only expect to find *hamas*. That's what Habakkuk didn't see. Alas, that's what often times we don't see.

I am in a presbytery. The history of our presbytery over the last 25 years is basically a long pattern of dramatic growth through church splits. If you look at the family tree of the churches in our presbytery almost every single church is a split from one of the other churches. We're Presbyterians all right. There has been more rancor, more bitterness, more intellectual *hamas* in our midst than I'd like to recount. Part of the reason for that is that we are like the brilliant Sunday school student, the front row pupil in the classical school or, God forbid, the I-already-know-the-answers student in the theological seminary classroom who knows all of the answers. He's got God pegged. He knows exactly what the system is. We become an awful lot like Habakkuk. We model

---

[6] Cited in Thomas MacGuidrie, *Habakkuk: A Preacher's Commentary* (Edinburgh: William Blackwood, 1934), 34.

ourselves very much after the Babylonians.

I had an opportunity to meet the king and wanted to say to him, "You know, there is an answer in the Middle East." It's the same answer that Habakkuk had to come to and ultimately does by chapter three after he marches through a series of woes, the *woes of plunder* in chapter two, verses six through eight, and *exploitation* in chapter two, verses nine through 11, and *ruthlessness* in chapter two, verses 12 through 14, and *cruelty* in verses 15 through 17 and *idolatry* in verses 18 through 20. After all the woes and only then, he finally comes to the end of himself and has nowhere to go but the gospel. He despairs of his own competency. He rids himself of his preconceived ideas. He does not abandon his theology because, as we can see, the Shigionoth is rich and full of theology—three great stanzas: chapter three, verses one through seven; chapter two, verses eight through 15 and chapter three, verses 16 to the end; each one of which is divided into three parts declaring the richness and the fullness of God's providential purposes throughout all of history. He mentions the glories of God as showing up in Edom and Cushan, verse three and seven, against the Amorites. He shows how God ultimately crushes the Canaanite pantheon in verse eight, and overthrows the Egyptians in verses eight through 10, and again in verse 15. This glorious vision of the whole history of redemption in which God is God and man marvels at the mysteries of his grace is the story of Habakkuk when he finally rids himself of his preconceived ideas of God.
And Habakkuk is brought to repentance.

The horror of Islam is that it has no need of repentance, which is the same horror that too easily creeps into many sessions, churches, and presbyteries from whence we show our Babylonish hearts. God answers Habakkuk and gently leads him to the place where he despairs of his competency, comes to the end of everyone of his pat answers and, in the end, has to simply cry out, "Oh Lord, in the midst of the years, revive it. In the midst of the years make it known in wrath remember mercy,"(Hab. 3:2). "God the Lord, is my strength; he makes my feet like the deer's; he makes me tread on my high places," (Hab. 3:19).

In this day when Babylonish ideologies are cloaked in high sounding rhetoric and fine, praiseworthy sentiment, may we, above all people, be quick to repent, to run to the mercy seat, to see Jesus as our only competency, our only hope, our only recourse. May we, of all people, show forth to a watching world that it is our repentance, not our ready answer that marks us as disciples of the sovereign King.

I did have a chance to say something like that to Vice President

Cheney. He chuckled. I didn't. As Mark Twain said, "Can't depend on your eyes when your imagination is out of focus." May God refocus us? As we consider these worldviews askew; they are all askew because of a refusal to run to the mercy seat, to lay hold of horns of the altar. May we not only see the error of *their* ways, may we see *ours* and cry out, "Oh Lord,…in the midst of the years revive it; in the midst of the years make it known; in wrath remember mercy," (Hab. 3:2).

Oh Father, I do pray for the myriads, the thousands, the tens of thousands and the millions who are shackled by the ideologies of this poor fallen world. Having seen throngs in Amman, in Baghdad, in Sulaimaniya, and in Jakarta, Oh Lord Jesus, my heart even now cries out for those thousands who are shackled by an Islam that has reduced their understanding of you, the most high sovereign God to a series of narrow propositions.

Father, we thank you that you do reveal yourself propositionally in your Word. But we thank you, too, that your glory and your majesty are beyond our imagining and that in your presence we are reduced to the place of crying out only, "Holy, holy, holy, Lord God almighty."
I pray that you would embolden us to go forth into this poor, fallen world with a message of hope, the message that there is a fall, that man is made in the very image of God, that repentance is a very real and substantial hope because Jesus Christ has come and paid the penalty for our hamas.

I pray, Lord God, that this gospel would go forth with abounding grace to the ends of the earth and so we cry, "Lord Jesus, sweep Iraq into your domain. Might you have Jordan as your own fiefdom? And bring all the islands of Indonesia into your dominion Lord Jesus, we pray." And use us, send us as we go forth leaving behind our Babylonish hearts for we pray this in Jesus' name.
Amen.

Chapter 4

Here I Stand:
An Historical, Biblical, & Missiological
View of Islam

Anees Zaka[1]

In 1521, Martin Luther was brought before the Diet of Worms and Charles the fifth, Emperor of the Holy Roman Empire, to defend the recent Protestant Reformation. Luther's response to the Diet, first given in Latin and then repeated in German, shook the world, infuriated Charles the fifth, and roused fellow reformers:

> Unless I am convinced by the testimony of the Holy Scriptures or by evident reason—for I can believe neither pope nor councils alone, as it is clear that they have erred repeatedly and contradicted themselves—I consider myself convicted by the testimony of Holy Scripture, which is my basis; my conscience is captive to the Word of God. Thus I cannot and will not recant, because acting against one's conscience is neither safe nor sound. God help me. Amen.[2]

---

[1]   Anees Zaka D. Min. is an ordained minister in the Presbyterian Church in America, Director of Church Without Walls, and President of the Biblical Institute for Islamic Studies in Philadelphia, PA.
[2]   Cited in Heiko Oberman, *Luther: Man Between God and the Devil*, trans.

Does history repeat itself? Yes indeed.

Since September 11, 2001, we have been hearing many different voices expressing many different ideas concerning Islam. Politicians and writers across the globe have gone to great lengths to persuade us that Islam and Christianity are *not* all that different. But is this the truth about Islam? People claim to love and seek Truth. Truth is so encompassing, so brilliantly complex, and so elegant in its harmony and coherence that it surpasses the full comprehension of any mortal.

*Qur'an*ic Islam claims to be the faith of Truth. Islam represents itself as a cousin of Judaism and Christianity and the champion of uncompromising monotheism, with Allah as its sole object of worship. But is this the truth about Islam? In order to uncover the truth about Islam—to understand Islam from a historical, biblical, and missiological point-of-view—I will divide my lecture in the following manner: First, Islam according to the scholars; Second, five essential assumptions of the Islamic worldview; Third, the self-image of the Muslim community—how Muslims see themselves; Fourth, Islam according to the Reformed Christians—Martin Luther, John Calvin, and Jonathan Edwards; Fifth, Islam according to the *Qur'an;* and, finally, Islam according to the Scriptures.

ISLAM DEFINED BY THE SCHOLARS

Bernard Lewis speaks of Islam in these words:

> The word Islam is used with at least three different meanings. Islam means the religion taught by the prophet Muhammad....Islam is the subsequent development of this religion through tradition and through the work of the great Muslim jurists and theologians....In the third meaning, Islam is the counterpart not of Christianity but rather of Christendom, not what the Muslims believe or were expected to believe but what they actually did. In other words, Islamic civilizations known to us in history.[3]

Ninian Smart says, "Islam is, as it were, a sandwich. At the top is the theology and refined spirituality of the religious elite, at the bottom the local customs into which Islam integrates. In the middle is the world of

---

Eileen Walliser-Schwarzbart (1982; New York: Doubleday Books, 1992), 39.
   [3]   Bernard Lewis, *Race and Color in Islam* (New York: Harper & Row, 1979), 6-7.

characteristic Islam—the mosque, the Koran and the law.[4]

From this we understand that Islam is a religion that applies differently to different categories of people in any Muslim society. There is one Islam for the *ulama* (teachers of Islamic law), while there is another Islam for the unlearned peasant. There is one Islam for worshippers with its detailed rituals, while there is another Islam that includes local customs concerning events for which there are not prescribed ceremonies: veneration at shrines of holy men, commemoration of the dead, circumcision, return from the *hajj* or the opening of a new house or business. Islam **idealized** is the religion of the theologian. Islam **realized** is the religion of the extraordinary, and Islam **personalized** is the religion of the believer.

Another definition of Islam is found in Charles J. Adams.

Morphologically Islam is a verbal noun, the infinitive of a verb meaning 'to accept,' 'to submit,' or perhaps 'to surrender. In contemporary theological language the word that most nearly renders its sense is 'commitment.' The verbal quality of the word should be emphasized; by its very form, it conveys a feeling of action and ongoingness, not of something that is once and for all finished and static. Hence, rather than 'commitment' it might still better be translated as 'committing' in order to underline the continued renewal and repetition of man's bowing to his Creator that it implies. In its most basic meaning, Islam is the name of a relationship between men and their Allah in which men self-consciously and reverently commit, submit, or surrender themselves anew with each moment to the highest reality they are capable of apprehending.[5]

In other words, Islam is a complete way of life. It is a *deen* (religion) and *donia* (earthly life full of every pleasure). Thus, Islam acknowledges no separation between the sacred and the secular, the realm of Caesar and the realm of God). It is a religion, but it is also far more than the church in the West usually understands by that term.

---

[4]   Ninian Smart cited in Anees Zaka Siha, "Principles And Methods Of Church Growth In A North American Context," (Doctor of Ministry Project, Westminster Theological Seminary, Philadelphia, 1988), 35.
[5]   Charles J. Adams, ed., *A Reader's Guide to the Great Religions* (New York: Free Press, 1977), 407-09.

ASSUMPTIONS OF THE ISLAMIC WORLDVIEW

The essential assumptions of Islam may be summarized as follows. First, man is the summit of God's creation. He is the *Khalif* (vicegerent) of Allah on earth. Man can choose to conform to Allah's ordinances, where the rest of creation cannot. Man is theomorphic, sharing in the divine attributes of intelligence, will, and speech, but he is not created in God's image. He is not a sinner, but weak and forgetful. Through Allah's guidance and revelations, man can seek to overcome his imperfections. Therefore, he does not need to have a savior to redeem him from his sins. He can do it for himself, through Allah's help. Second, man is not sure of his eternal destiny. Conformity with Allah's will is thought to determine his destiny but does not give him assurance of eternal life. Third, Allah has revealed to man the right path to live, by means of his prophets (28 named in the *Qur'an*). Abraham was one of them who proclaimed that there was one creator Allah who was to be worshipped. Moses founded the law but limited its applications to one people (the Jews). Jesus (*Isa*) universalized Allah's word—but the messenger was worshipped instead of the message. Muhammad, as the seal of the prophets, set the record straight, and is therefore above all other messengers. Fourth, Islam as a system of beliefs is a re-statement of what Allah has said to man. But Islam is also a form of society embodying and elaborating that re-statement into action. Finally, the characteristic manifestation of Islam is the law, which is defined in the widest sense as a body of prescriptions for right action in every sphere of life.

THE SELF IMAGE OF THE MUSLIM *UMMA* (COMMUNITY)

What is the nature of Islam? What do Muslims believe to be the most fundamental features of their faith worldwide? First, Muslims believe that Islam is universal. Although proclaimed in Arabic to the Arabs of Muhammad's time, Islam is a religion for all mankind. They establish their claim on this *Qur'anic* verse: "We have not sent you but as mercy for all nations" (*Surah* 21:102). Muslims believe also that Islam is the only future hope for humanity, and its victory over other religions and cultures is assured because all men came from one community (*Umma*) without distinction of race, color, language, and culture. Second, Islam is comprehensive. It is not a mere creed, but is the basis of a complete way of life, not only for individuals, but for all nations as well. It has an economic, social, civil, criminal, and international legal system (*Ahamd*).

Islam is, in the third place, eternal. Muslim scholars believe that Islam is the one true religion of Allah. It is the religion, which God made known on the day when man first appeared on earth. In every age, in every country and among every people, all God-knowing and truth-loving men have believed this very religion (Islam). They were all Muslims, irrespective of whether they called their way Islam or something else (*Maududi*). Fourth, Islam is not a religion of the sword. Muslims are concerned to refute the allegation that Islam achieved its conversions at the point of a sword. Their theory of jihad often stresses the conditions that surround warfare "in the way of Allah" notably the requirement that it should be defensive. Warfare is, therefore, the lesser jihad, the greater jihad being the struggle against self which takes place within each devout Muslim. Muslims use the following *Qur'anic* indicators as the basis of their claim that Islam is not a religion of the sword:

- "And fight in the way of Allah against those who fight against you, and not aggressively; surely Allah does not love the aggressor" (*Surah* 2:190).

- "Let there be no compulsion in religion. The right Path has surely been made distinct from the wrong..." (*Surah* 2:256).

- "God will not change the condition of a people until they change what is in their hearts" (*Surah* 21:11).

These verses indicate two kinds of *jihad,* which I mentioned earlier: first, *jihad* against people who are the enemy of the way of Allah; and, second, *jihad* against one's self to reach the way of Allah spiritually (*Azzam* 63-70).

Finally, you should know that Islam views itself as *rational, realistic, harmonious*, and *misunderstood. Islam is rational.* Commentators and Muslim scholars stress that Islam is not anti-scientific. "O my Lord! Advance me in knowledge" (*Surah* 20:114). They say that there is nothing in the *Qur'an* that is against reason, and nothing that can be proved wrong. None of its injunctions are unjust— nothing is misleading (*Maududi*). *Islam is realistic.* Muslim writers argue that the religion of Islam accepts human nature as it is without damaging it by describing it as sinful, as the people of the book (Jews and Christians) believe. Islam proclaims that polygamy is the most balanced approach to social relationships between men and women. Through the institution of polygamy, divine guidance has steered a middle course between the two extremes that were devoid of rationality, decency, and justice. It is a balanced way between celibacy and promiscuity (*Qutb*).

Islam also views itself as harmonious. Again, Muslim scholars and teachers emphasize the fact that through Islam alone, harmony can be achieved both for the individual and society. They claim that Islam reconciles the conflicts of people and nations, faith and science, the material and the spiritual, the terrestrial and the transcendent. They claim that Islam has a twofold objective in this regard: one, for an individual's life, it aims at making a just and sufficient provision to teach him or her how to live a clean, decent life, and two, for the community, it provides the basic principles of its life socially, economically, spiritually to direct it towards the enhancement of progress and civilization. Islam is a religion for individuals and communities, without making any distinction between them. Therefore, in reaching Muslims for the Gospel, we must also bear in mind this concept of reaching both the individual and the community (*Maududi*).

Finally, *Islam is misunderstood.* Almost 99% of Muslims believe that their religion is misunderstood, especially in the West. Therefore, one can see how Muslims have rejected the Gospel because of westerners who seek to downgrade Islam as a religion. Thus, we believe that to reach Muslims for Christ, we must open ourselves to them and hear their point of view concerning their religion. It is clear from our experience with them that the right approach to Muslim evangelism is an educational one. Because they misunderstand the teaching of the Gospel as we also misunderstand Islam, a teaching ministry for both Christians and Muslims is very much needed to remove the misunderstanding from both sides (*Qutb*).

ISLAM ACCORDING TO THE HISTORIC REFORMED CHRISTIAN

First, let us consider the German Reformer Martin Luther. In expounding Daniel 11, Luther noted that among others, the prophet Daniel was referring to the Muslim Turks, who at the time were invading Europe. "In the latter part of their reign," wrote Luther, "when rebels have become completely wicked, a stern-faced king, a master of intrigue will arise. He will become very strong, but not by his own power....He will cause deceit to prosper and he will consider himself superior. When he feels secure, he will destroy many and take his stand against the

Prince of princes. Yet he will be destroyed, but not by human power,"[6] (Daniel 11:23-25). Luther wrote further that the "two regimes, that of the Pope and that of the Turk, are...antichrist."[7]

In his comments on Matthew 24:24-26, Luther noted that Christ warned about false prophets coming from the desert—most certainly an illusion that included Muhammad.[8] From 1 John 2:18-22 and 4:1-3, the German wrote, "Who is the liar? It is the man who denies that Jesus is the Christ. Such a man is the antichrist—he denies the   Father and the Son," that the Mohammedans deny both the Fatherhood of God and the Deity of Christ—hence they are liars. They testify against the truth of God's word.[9]

Luther also observed that the Muslim Turks wanted to "eradicate the Christians." He also concluded that Islam was God's judgment upon Roman corruption, a rod of correction for our sin. Islam, he asserted, is the religion of "natural man," which explains its appeal and success to mankind. He called on the church to pray and repent, as a means to stand up to Islam, as well as to go back to the Word, the only news of God's grace for men in despair.[10]

John Calvin, the Geneva Reformer, in a sermon on Daniel 7, maintained that Muhammad was one of the "two horns of the antichrist." He also put forward the theory that Muslim Turks were the little horn that sprang up from the beast and Islam was one of the two legs of the later Roman Empire. Additionally, Calvin wrote that Muhammad "allow men to brutally chastise their wives and thus corrupt the conjugal love and fidelity which binds the husband to the wife...Muhammad allowed full scope of various lusts—by permitting a man to have a number of wives...Muhammad invented a new form of religion."[11]

Commenting on 2 Thessalonians 2:3-12, Calvin said, "the sect of Muhammad was like a raging overflow, which in its violence tore away about half of the church." "The Turks," he explained, "have a mere idol in place of God." In his magisterial *Institutes of the Christian Religion,* Calvin writes, "So today the   Turks, although they proclaim at the top of their lungs that the Creator of Heaven and earth is God, still, while

---

[6]   Martin Luther cited in Peter Hammond, *The Greatest Century of Reformation* (Howard Place, South Africa: Christian Liberty Books, 2006), 191.
[7]   Ibid.
[8]   Ibid.
[9]   Ibid., 191-92.
[10]   Ibid.
[11]   Ibid.

repudiating Christ, substitute an idol in the place of the true God."[12]

Preaching from 2 Timothy 1:3, Calvin explained: "The Turks at this day, can allege and say for themselves: 'We serve God from our ancestors!' It is a good while ago since Muhammad gave them the cup of his devilish dreams to drink, and they got drunk with them. It is about a thousand years since those cursed hellhounds were made drunk with their follies. Let us be wise and discreet! Otherwise we shall be like the Turks and Heathens!"[13]

Calvin also pointed out that the reign of the antichrist will be destroyed by the Word of God.

> Paul does not think that Christ will accomplish this in a single moment. Christ will scatter the darkness in which antichrist will reign, by the rays which he will emit before his coming—just as the sun, before becoming visible to us, chases away the darkness of the night with its bright light. The victory of the Word will therefore be seen in the World. For the breath of his mouth means simply his Word, as in Isaiah 11:4, the passage to which Paul appears to be alluding.

Finally, Calvin concluded that Islam is not to be compared to the True Religion, according to the Word of God. Islam is, however, to be compared to the teachings of the Pharisees, or to the papal doctrines added to the Gospels. Calvin insisted that the *Qur'an* contained distorted biblical stories and rabbinical traditions. Islamic teaching, therefore, is a departure from the pure and simple Word of God of the Old and New Testaments.[14]

Finally, one quotation from Jonathan Edwards will suffice to show his learned opinion of Islam. In his *A History of the Work of Redemption* we read:

> The two great works of the devil which he wrought against the Kingdom of Christ are his Anti-Christ [Romish or Papal] and Mahometan [Muslim or Islamic] kingdoms, which have been and still are two kingdoms of great strength. Both together swallow up the ancient Roman Empire; the Papal kingdom of

---

[12]   John Calvin, *The Institutes of the Christian Religion,* ed. John T. McNeill, trans. Ford Lewis Battles (Philadelphia: Westminster Press, 1960), 2.6.4.
[13]   Hammond, *The Greatest Century,* 193.
[14]   Ibid.

Antichrist swallowing up the Western empire, and Satan's Mahometan kingdom the Eastern empire. In the book of Revelation, it is in the destruction of these that the glorious victory of Christ at the introduction of the glorious times of the church, will mainly consist...."[15]

ISLAM ACCORDING TO THE *QUR'AN*

Next I wish to set before you in chart form what the *Qur'an* says about Islam.

The religion accepted by Allah	*Surah* 3:19-20, 84; 110:2
A better religion, requiring man to submit to Allah	2:112; 4:125
Bowing to Allah, no one else	6:14, 71, 125; 39:12, 22, 24
Believing in Allah and his messenger (Muhammad)	9:74
Muhammad's way	109:6
Worshipping Allah	10:104-5
A revelation sent down with the knowledge of Allah	11:14
Allah's favor on men that bow to his will	16:81
Allah's favor upon you	49:17
Submitting your will to Allah, who is one	22:34; 27:31, 42, 81
Coming to Allah in full submission	49:14
Bowing before the lord of the worlds	40:66
Calling me to Allah to bow	41:33
Believing in the signs of Muhammad and bowing your will to him	43:69
A chosen religion by Allah for you	5:3; 24:55
Holding fast to Allah	22:78
The religion of the prophets	42:13

---

[15] Ibid.

The religion of Truth	9:29, 33; 48:28; 6:19
The most trustworthy religion	2:256; 31:22
The right religion	12:40; 30:30; 45:18
The word of Allah	9:6
Desired by unbelievers	15:2
An invitation to all	61:7

ISLAM ACCORDING TO THE SCRIPTURES

By way of comparison, here are the characteristics of *Qur'anic* Islam and biblical Christianity.

Human effort	*Surah* 3:132	Work of God	John 3:5
Tradition of Men	Sunnah	God's Grace	2 Peter 3:18
Earthly Dress	33:59	Heavenly Dress	Isaiah 61:10
Regulated Life	17:78	Radiant Life	Matthew 5:16
Repressed Conscience	58:2-3	Rebuilt Character	Matthew 7:24
Fraternity of Ummah	2:143	Fellowship with Christ	Luke 24:32
Separation from Allah	42:49-50	Union with Yahweh	John 1:12
Direction	4:58-59	Discipleship	John 8:31-32
Submission	4:34-35	Service	1 Timothy 6:18
Limited Sacrifice	47:36-37	Living Sacrifice	Romans 12:1
Walk Alone	74:44-47	Walk with Christ	Colossians 2:6

Physical Warfare	9:73		Spiritual Warfare	1 Timothy 6:12
Recitation and Ritual	22:28-30		Running a Race	Hebrews 12:1
Cultural Imperialism	3:110		Spiritual Victory	1 John 5:4
Immortality with Companions	37:45-49		Immortality with Christ	John 17:3

- *Qur'an*ic Islam is submission to Allah, as a slave submits to his master. It is not a relationship between man and God.
- *Qur'an*ic Islam is to bow before Allah out of fear and not out of love. It is not fellowship between man and his Creator.
- *Qur'an*ic Islam is a religion of good works, generally defined as physical acts of worship and public devotion. It is not a union between man and God.
- *Qur'an*ic Islam is what you do for Allah, not what Allah does for you. It is not a personal experience of man with God.

Simply put, from a biblical point-of-view, Islam is *not* a religion of God's redeeming love; God's forgiveness; God's redemption; God's mercy or kindness to sinners; God's compassion for sinners; God's truth in it's teaching and living; God's peace for the human heart; God's freedom of thought for man as His image bearer; God's saving grace; God's justice and fairness to all; God's holiness; God's eternal hope; God's holy revelation (Hebrews 1:1-3). Rather, Islam *is* a religion of the sword; fighting and killing; falsehood (2 Peter 2:1-3); an anti-Christ (1 John 4:1-6); deception (1 John 2:20-27); submission, not peace; intolerance; hatred, revenge, and invasion.[16]

A Sufi prayer illustrates the truth of this biblical Christian evaluation of Islam and strongly pleas for Christians to present the good news of justification, adoption, sanctification, and glorification to Muslims wherever they may be found.

---

[16] Anees Zaka and Diane Coleman, *The Truth about Islam* (Phillipsburg, NJ: P&R Publishing Co., 2004), 20-29.

I am truly bankrupt, O God. I stand before the door of Thy riches. Truly I have great sins—forgive me for Thine own sake. Truly I am a stranger, a sinner, a humble slave who has nothing but forgetfulness and disobedience to present to Thee. My sins are as the sands, without number. Forgive me and pardon me. Remove my transgressions and undertake my cause. Truly my heart is sick, but Thou are able to heal it. My condition, O God, is such that have no good work. My evil deeds are many, and my provision of obedience is small. Speak to the fire of my heart, as Thou didst in the case of Abraham, "be cool for my servant."[17]

CONCLUSION

As a conclusion to this chapter I wish to present a Reformed Christian missiological view of Islam and how then we can reach them for Christ. At this point I will draw on the labors of the late apologist Cornelius Van Til. First, if we are to effectively and faithfully challenge Islam we must *not compromise Christ.* "If Christ is to be presented to [Muslims] as a challenge to their thinking and living," wrote Van Til, "then he must be offered without compromise." Second, we must *challenge them to surrender to Christ through faith not add Christ to their list of good, even great prophets.* "The natural man is not challenged to make his every thought captive to the obedience of Christ," explained Van Til. "The natural man is merely asked to add the wisdom and work of Christ to that which man has in and of himself." Third, Christians must *hold forth the Scriptures to Muslins as necessary, authoritative, perspicuous, and sufficient.* As Van Til stated: "The basic structure of Christian theology is simple. Its every teaching should be taken from the Scriptures of the Old and New Testaments as being the words of prophets and apostles spoken on the authority of Jesus Christ, the Son of God and Son of Man, the Savior of sinners."[18]

We must never forget, "As Christians, we find what we believe expressed in the Bible as the word of God. From the Bible, we have taken our doctrines of God, man, Christ, salvation and the last things. As

---

[17]   Ibid., 173-74.
[18]   Cited in Anees Zaka and Alfred A. Z. Siha, eds., "It is Written! The Use of Cornelius Van Til's Apologetics for Doing Missions Among Muslims," Church Without Walls, 2005), no page numbers.

reformed Christians, we wish to show [Muslims] that it is reformed theology that they need." We do this best by *pointing out the differences between Christianity and Islam*: Two final quotes from Van Til flesh out this point: 1)"Basic to all the differences between the Christian and the non Christian views of life is the fact that Christians worship and serve the Creator, while non Christians worship and serve the creature;" 2)"Because of the redemption of Christ and its application in our hearts by the Holy Spirit, Christians have learned, in principle, to worship and serve the Creator more than the creature."[19]

Finally, let me challenge Christians to be *grounded in your Christian faith.* Jonathan Edwards was surely correct when he wrote, "We know that there are many adversaries to the Gospel and its truths. Unless we be well informed concerning divine things, how shall we be able to defend ourselves?"[20] We must *present the simple message of the gospel to Muslims with authority*: "I have found that when I present the simple message of the Gospel of Jesus Christ with authority, quoting the very Word of God, that the Holy Spirit takes that message and drives it supernaturally into the human heart."[21] And, we must *build our teaching to Muslims on the Scriptures.* The late James Montgomery Boice observed: "I have seen many human theories and many popular fads come and go. But the Word of God remains like a rock in the midst of raging storms, treacherous offshore currents, and nearly invisible quick sands. It is good [that] it does, because only the one who builds on this rock will truly stand forever."[22] With all this *Christians should show Muslims their need for Christ*: "It could be," wrote J. I. Packer, "that we will see massive inroads into the West by Islam. As a religion, it is not suffering from the distress of the post-Christian West. Islam has a high morality and despises Christians for their post-modern condition. Muslims feel they are God's people for the 21st Century. Islam will be a major challenge for Christians because it is integrated, homogenous, and morally strict. The tragedy is that it is an anti-Jesus and hardhearted with no Gospel. Muslims don't know the love of God in Christ Jesus our Lord. Christians will have to find a way to meet the challenge and evangelize them, showing them that through Christ, we have something

---

[19]   Ibid.
[20]   Jonathan Edwards in "An Educational Newsletter," Church Without Walls (Winter/Spring 2002).
[21]   Billy Graham in "An Educational Newsletter," 3.
[22]   James Montgomery Boice in "An Educational Newsletter," 3.

they desperately need."[23] Finally, in our approach to Muslims, we must *explain our Biblical presupposition to our Muslim hearers*. "It is only the Christian presupposition," argues Morton Smith, "that provides a rational basis to account for the facts of the universe and of mankind. All other proposals are irrational."[24]

And, finally, let us rehearse just a few of the transcendent truths of the Holy Scriptures, ever keeping in mind how they pertain to every tribe, tongue, nation, and, we may confidently say, every religion.

"The kingdoms of the world become the Kingdom of our Lord and of His Christ, and He shall reign for ever and ever." Revelation 11: 15

"All nations will come and worship before you, for your righteous acts have been revealed." Revelation 15 : 4

"The desert tribes will bow before Him and His enemies will lick the dust... All kings will bow down to Him and all nations will serve Him." Psalm 72:9- 11

RECOMMENDED READING ON ISLAM

Anderson, Norman. *Islam in the Modern World: A Christian Response* Downers Grove, IL: Inter-Varsity, 1990.

Chapman, Colin. *Cross & Crescent: Responding the challenge of Islam.* Downers Grove, IL: Inter- Varsity Press, 1995.

Hammond, Peter. *The Greatest Century of Reformation.* Cape Town, South Africa: Christian Liberty Books, 2006.

McDowell, Bruce and Anees Zaka. *Muslims and Christians at the Table.* Phillipsburg, NJ: P&R Publishing, 1999.

---

[23]   James I. Packer in "An Educational Newsletter," 3.
[24]   Morton H. Smith, *Systematic Theology,* 2 vols. (Greenville, SC: Greenville Presbyterian Theological Seminary Press, 1994), 1:39.

Warraq, Ibn. *Why I am not a Muslim.* Amherst, NY: Prometheus Books, 1995.

Masood, Steven. *Into The Light: A Young Muslim's Search for Truth.* Publisher. Waynesboro, GA: Authentic Lifestyle, 2002.

Massod, Steven. *The Bible and The Qur'an: A Question of Integrity* Waynesboro, GA: O.M. Publishing, 2001.

Spencer, Robert. *The Politically Incorrect Guide to Islam.* Boca Raton, FL: Regnery Publishing, Inc., 2005.

Zaka, Anees and Diane Coleman. *Cry of the Heart and Quest of the Mind.* Philadelphia: Church Without Walls, 2006.

Zaka, Anees and Diane Coleman. *The Truth About Islam.* Phillipsburg, NJ: P&R Publishing, 2004.

Chapter 5

Roman Catholicism: A View Into Its World

Mark A. Herzer[1]

INTRODUCTION

What do we mean when we say that something is Roman Catholic? The words mean different things to different people. Most in the Reformed community have in mind pre-Vatican II Catholicism. Unfortunately, we often wrestle against a notion of Catholicism that does not adequately take into account Vatican II. It is as if the second Vatican did little to nothing. After all, Catholicism is still reputed to be *semper idem*, always the same. In fact, this has been the seductive allure for many ex-protestants who have made their way to Rome. With all the vicissitudes in modern evangelicalism, Catholicism appeared to be a safe haven.[2]

These recent converts to Catholicism offer various reasons for their defection. They believe they are going to a richer and more traditional church; there is continuity with the past. Other people are

---

[1]   Mark Herzer PhD is Pastor of Christ Covenant Presbyterian Church (PCA) in Hatboro, PA.
[2]   The growing number of defections is alarming; for example, see Scott and Kimberly Hahn, *Rome Sweet Home: Our Journey to Catholicism* (San Francisco: Ignatius Press, 1993). For an excellent critique, see Kim Riddlebarger, "No Place Like Rome? Why are Evangelicals Joining the Catholic Church?," in *Roman Catholicism: Evangelical Protestants Analyze What Divides and Unites Us*, ed. John Armstrong (Chicago: Moody Press, 1994), 220-243.

drawn to its supposed stability; this church has staying power, they maintain. Some converts I've read find refuge in the "infallible" teaching of the *Magisterium*. And finally, some have found a definitive and authoritative answer and are no longer mired in myriads of opinions. Many perceive the Roman Church to be the only institution that can withstand the forces of modernity and liberalism. It is also not uncommon to hear some disillusioned evangelicals say something like, "At least, you won't get any of those silly worship services that plague the evangelical churches. You never know what you're going to get in those Protestant services." Quite frequently, many are enamored with the mystery and majesty of the liturgy, cathedrals, and art. One person even wept uncontrollably when he walked into the Roman Catholic church because the experience of its beauty overwhelmed him.[3] All of this has wooed and wowed many dejected Protestants. They have found a safe haven in Rome. They have finally arrived; they have come home!

The yearning for that safe haven is understandable, but I am convinced (and will seek to prove) that the supposed security they so energetically espouse is the biggest deception in modern church history. The reason for this strong protest has very much to do with how we answer the question, "What is Roman Catholicism?" Scott Hahn and other defectors have fled to a kind of Catholicism that simply does not exist except in their own minds. Roman Catholicism is battling within herself and it remains to be seen what she will become.

WILL THE REAL ROMAN CATHOLIC CHURCH PLEASE STAND UP?

In this section, I will argue that the second Vatican Council (1962-1965) so infected Roman Catholicism that she can no longer claim, "ALWAYS THE SAME" (*semper idem*). One Catholic theologian summarized it this way, "There are some events in church history so decisive that they set the agenda for an entire historical era. For Catholic ecclesiology the second Vatican Council seems to have been such an event."[4]

---

[3]   Some of these anecdotes can be found on the Coming Home Network, http://www.chnetwork.org/converts.htm .
[4]   Avery Dulles, *The Resilient Church: The Necessity and Limits of Adaptation* (New York: Doubleday & Company, Inc., 1977), 1.

Under Pope John XXIII, Vatican II met to modernize the church.[5] They wanted to revitalize the church and speak to the culture in a relevant manner.[6] Before this Pope, a stifling conservative trend controlled Catholicism and some say that this repression was bound to unravel. One writer said that Vatican II "did not spring Athena-like from the head of the conciliar Zeus. What the Council did was to summon into the mainstream of Catholic life and theology ideas, activities, and aspirations which had, during the previous hundred years, had a suspect, and therefore precarious, existence in the Church. Most of the men who educated the Church in council in the early 1960s had been victims of the extremely narrow standards of orthodoxy which pervaded the Roman dicasteries."[7] Therefore, it is no wonder the changes in Vatican II were so drastic. This turned out to be a very different ecumenical council.

The Second Vatican Council is different from the many ecumenical councils that have preceded it in at least two respects. First, it did not result from either external persecution or internal heresy. Second, for the first time in conciliar history, the documents which Vatican II developed officially embraced mutually incompatible theologies.[8]

Of the many changes (new mass in the vernacular, more collegiality between the *magisterium* and the bishops, less centralized power, more lay involvement, etc.), the most disturbing one is its understanding of salvation outside the church. A form of "universalism" now plagues Roman Catholicism. This poisonous pill will either kill Catholicism or Rome will have to admit that she erred in this council and

---

[5]   Vatican II had more delegates than any other ecumenical council. Vatican I had 737 while Vatican II had 2600. The number was close to 3,000 when you count all the experts on hand to assist and participate. See Richard McBrien, *Catholicism,* 2 vols. (Minneapolis: Winston, 1980), 2:657-658.

[6]   Dulles, *The Resilient Church,* 1, 63. That this is the case is undisputed since the Pope himself declared this. See R. F. Trisco and J. A. Komonchak, "Vatican Council II," in *The New Catholic Encyclopedia,* ed. Berard L. Marthaler, 2nd ed., vol. 14 (Washington, D.C.: Gale in association with The Catholic University of America, 2003), 407-418.

[7]   Gabriel Daly, *Transcendence and Immanence: A Study in Catholic Modernism and Integralism* (Oxford: Clarendon Press, 1980), 220-221. A "dicastery" is "one of the official congregations of the Holy See, e.g., the Congregation for Religious and Secular Institutes, through which the Pope conducts the regular administration of the universal Church" (John A. Hardon, *Modern Catholic Dictionary* [Garden City, NY: Doubleday & Company, Inc., 1980]).

[8]   D. F. Wells, *Revolution in Rome* (Downers Grove, IL: InterVarsity Press, 1972), 27.

must purge this whole line of thinking from its decrees. What then did the council teach?

In the *Lumen Gentium* 16 (Dogmatic Constitution of the Church, hereafter *LG*)[9] we are told what the destinies are for those who have not believed the gospel: "those who have not yet accepted the gospel are related to the people of God in various ways." This would include the Jews as well as other people who have rejected the gospel. They are not cut off from salvation because they do not accept the gospel but in some remote way they "are related to the People of God in various ways." Furthermore, it explains that God has a plan for other religions: "But the plan of salvation also embraces those who acknowledge the Creator, and among these the Moslems are first (*inter quos imprimis Musulmanos*)...." Accordingly, for Vatican II Romanism, a certain plan of salvation is available to them because they acknowledge a Creator. But does not the Bible make it clear that acknowledging the Creator is the minimal instinct of a human being? Salvation does not come from knowing the Creator, *but* knowing the Creator as Savior through Jesus Christ.

Similar doctrines are taught in the "Declarations on the Church's Relation to Non-Christian Religions" (*Nostra Aetate,* hereafter *NA*). Jews, Hindus, Buddhists, and Muslims are held in *high regard.* They are not viewed as idolaters but as simply being less illumined. The Roman Church "rejects nothing of those things which are true and holy in these religions" (*NA* 2). These Roman Catholic divines do not see pagan religions as expressions of human idolatry but rather as benevolent human attempts at knowing God.

We Protestants are called "separated fellow Christians" (Decree of Ecumenism [*Unitatis Redintegratio,* hereafter *UR*], 4). We are nonetheless called brothers and sisters (*UR* 3). In the Tridentine decrees, we were condemned for our beliefs, but in these new decrees, we are viewed as erring brothers. We Protestants may like these declarations but we must also note that Muslims, Buddhists, Hindus, and Atheists have all been given a positive place and purpose. They have opened the door to almost everyone.

---

[9]   The words *Lumen Gentium* (LG) are the first two words of the official Latin text of the Second Vatican documents. LG was accepted on Nov. 21, 1964. I will be using the Second Vatican Council text from Norman P. Tanner S. J., ed., *Decrees of the Ecumenical Councils*, 2 vols. (Washington, D.C.: Georgetown University Press, 1990), 2:816-1135.

Those who have not yet accepted the gospel (*evangelium nondum acceperunt*) are related to God's people and all religions that acknowledge the Creator are embraced in God's salvation somehow. The next question is, "What about our very secular friends who haven't heard? What about those people who haven't ever been exposed to the gospel?" This is answered with, "There are those who without any fault do not know anything about Christ or his church, yet who search for God with a sincere heart and, under the influence of grace, try to put into effect the will of God as known to them through the dictate of conscience: these too can obtain eternal salvation" (*LG* 16).

The same document goes on to explain what happens to secular people who try to be good. If they are trying to be good, then certainly divine grace must be operative in their lives. "Nor does divine Providence deny the helps that are necessary for salvation to those who, through no fault of their own, have not yet attained to the express recognition of God yet who strive, not without divine grace, to lead an upright life." Let me translate this for you. The Second Vatican Council is teaching us that some people strive very hard to be good, but have not "attained to the express recognition of God" which means they do not even know if God exists. They may even be atheists or those who have not explicitly stated that they believed in God.[10] To them, the Council states, God would not deny what is needed for their salvation. Explicit faith in Jesus Christ is not necessary. This goes a step further than the 1863 Encyclical ("*Quanto conficiamur moerore*") since Pope Pius IX (1846-1878) condemned those "who are obstinate … and who persistently separate themselves from the unity of the Church, and from the Roman Pontiff." Yet, notwithstanding the condemnation, he did state that those who "labor in invincible ignorance of our holy religion…can,

---

[10]   Aloys Grillmeier does raise some probing questions on this 16th article of LG. "All that is affirmed is that God's salutary grace in not denied them. How does this grace affect salvation? Is salvation possible within the bounds of this inculpable, theoretical atheism, say, by means of a theism implicit in the moral life under the influence of grace, which also implies revelation and faith? Or does grace liberate them from such atheism — and when? The text does not answer these questions. But if salutary grace is possible apart from the explicit preaching of the gospel, the first possibility cannot be excluded. In any case, the moral attitude of such atheists is termed a praeparatio evangelica. The precise way in which the grace of God uses these presuppositions to take hold of men is not described. But an inward guidance is supposed, as follows from the words of the text, which speaks of 'goodness' and 'truth' as the gift of him 'who enlightens all men so that they may *finally (tandem)* have life'." See Herbert Vorgrimler, ed., *Commentary on the Documents of Vatican II*, 5 vols. (New York: Herder and Herder, 1967), 1:184.

by the operating power of divine light and grace, attain eternal life...."[11]
It is interesting, and I think important to note, that the Second Vatican declaration avoids all the condemnations and affirms only the possibilities of salvation.

One Catholic theologian put it this way, "Lumen Gentium recognizes that salvation is possible even apart from explicit faith in Christ, or even apart from any religious faith at all."[12] Another writer confidently says, "Today, however, the Second Vatican Council has laid down that even the atheist has a genuine chance of salvation *so long as* he is true to the promptings of his own conscience."[13] Avery Dulles summarized the latter part of *LG* 16 in these words: "And the following sentence extends this principle to those who in good faith doubt or deny the existence of God. Such men may be in a hidden way living by the grace of God and of Christ...[and have a] real but unrecognized relationship to Christ as their Redeemer."[14]

This teaching is not restricted to *Lumen Gentium* 16, but it can also be found in *Ad Gentes* 7 ("Decree on the Missionary Activity of the Church"): "So, although God, through ways known to himself, can lead people who through no fault of their own are ignorant of the gospel, to that faith without which it is impossible to please him, nevertheless the church has both the obligation and the sacred right to evangelise." Somehow, God will mysteriously lead people to faith though they are ignorant of the gospel. Note, it does not say that He will mysteriously lead them to the knowledge of the gospel but rather simply to faith. In

---

[11]   H. Denzinger and A. Schönmetzer, ed., *Enchiridion Symbolorum, Definitionum et Declarationum De Rebus Fidei et Morum*, XXXIV ed. (Barcelona: Herder, 1967), 571 (§2866); it can also be found 771 (§3870); for a translation of most of Denzinger, see Hendricus Denzinger, *The Sources of Catholic Dogma*, 30th ed., trans. Roy J. Deferrari (Fitzwilliam, NH: Loreto Publications, 1955), 425.

[12]   Richard McBrien, "The Church (*Lumen Gentium*)," in *Modern Catholicism: Vatican II and After*, ed. Adrian Hastings (New York: Oxford University Press, 1991), 91.

[13]   Karl Rahner, "Theological Considerations on Secularization and Atheism," in *Theological Investigations*, vol. 11 (New York: The Seabury Press, 1974), 176.

[14]   Avery Dulles, *The Dimensions of the Church: A Postconciliar Reflection* (Westminster, Maryland: Newman Press, 1966), 47. The Protestant theologian David Wells summarized the Vatican position this way in *Revolution in Rome* (Downers Grove, IL: InterVarsity Press, 1972), 91: "...the Council did not exclude the possibility of an atheist's being saved. Philosophical atheism and an inarticulate Christianity may cohabit in the same man at the same time. Consciously and explicitly he may be an atheist; unconsciously and implicitly he may be a Christian."

Gaudium et Spes 19-22 (esp. the latter part of 22),[15] the Council develops a similar doctrine, though less explicit.[16] It speaks of God's grace "secretly at work" (interestingly, the reference to this statement takes us back to *LG* 16) and that "the holy Spirit offers everyone the possibility of sharing in this paschal mystery in a manner known to God" (*GS*, 22).

KARL RAHNER'S INFLUENCE

All these things we have just reviewed reveal Karl Rahner's unmistakable influence on the Second Vatican Council. Karl Rahner (1904-1984) was a brilliant theologian and philosopher (influenced by Heidegger) in the Roman Catholic Church who served as one of the advisors to the Vatican Council. This German Jesuit theologian is still considered to be one of the most influential theologians of the twentieth century.[17] He has tainted more of modern Catholicism than almost anyone else and "marked in a decisive way most of the questions debated in the Catholic Church during the period of Vatican II."[18] Another writer said that "the entire work and spirit of Vatican II was a vindication of Rahner's way of doing theology."[19] One can hardly deal with Catholicism without considering him. This typical assessment fairly summarizes Rahner's life: "A warm supporter of Christian unity, his was a voice often heard during and after Vatican II, much to the dismay of more conservative forces. For a time he was under a publications ban. Some, nevertheless, have called him the most important theologian since Aquinas, with an influence that extended beyond his own church."[20]

In order to understand why Rahner's influence is so disturbing, we will need to review some of his theological positions. First, Rahner was simply delighted with the Second Vatican Council and noted that the

---

[15] *Gaudium et Spes* is the "Pastoral Constitution on the Church in the World Today" (*Constitutio pastoralis de ecclesia in mundo huius temporis*).

[16] Cf. Karl Rahner, "Atheism and Implicit Christianity," in *Theological Investigations*, vol. 9 (New York: Herder and Herder, 1972), 147.

[17] Most recently, a companion guide was published to summarize this influence and teaching. See Declan Marmion and Mary E. Hines, ed., *The Cambridge Companion to Karl Rahner* (Cambridge: Cambridge University Press, 2005).

[18] See "Rahner, Karl," in *Dictionary of Christian Biography,* ed. Michael Walsh (Collegeville: The Liturgical Press, 2001).

[19] William A. Herr, *Catholic Thinkers in the Clear: Giants of Catholic Thought from Augustine to Rahner,* Basics of Christian Thought, vol. 2 (Chicago: The Thomas More Press, 1985), 259.

[20] J. D. Douglas, ed., *New 20th-Century Encyclopedia of Religious Knowledge*, 2nd ed. (Grand Rapids: Baker Book House, 1991), 693.

Council never positively declared that atheists would go to hell.[21] He had taught that there was such a thing as "anonymous Christianity."[22] This notion became one of the hallmarks of the Second Vatican Council. This is how Rahner defined his view: "Implicit Christianity—it could also be termed 'anonymous Christianity'—is what we call the condition of a man who lives on the one hand in a state of grace and justification, and yet on the other hand has not come into contact with the explicit preaching of the Gospel and is consequently not in a position to call himself a 'Christian'."[23] This might sound confusing because his view is quite sophisticated, but there is a simpler way of explaining it. I will explain it in theological terms, though his whole strategy is philosophically based. He believed that a great majority of people are "anonymous Christians" because they do not know that they are Christians. How could he say this as a Roman Catholic theologian? His reasoning goes something like this. God desires the salvation of all. Not all of fallen men had access to revealed religion, but they were nonetheless always religious. The OT reveals that there were those outside of revealed religion who knew God (Job). Therefore, religion beyond the reach of explicit revealed religion can be acceptable to God. That is to say, anyone outside of revealed religion can somehow possess a relationship with God in the context in which he finds himself. Furthermore, if we damn all those who have not heard the gospel or all those who are secular atheists, then God's powerful desire for the salvation of all would have been thwarted. But Christ has purchased

---

[21]   Karl Rahner, "Atheism and Implicit Christianity," 147.

[22]   Karl Rahner, "Christianity and the Non-Christian Religions," in *Theological Investigations,* vol. 5 (Baltimore: Helicon Press, 1966), 115-134; "Anonymous Christians," in *Theological Investigations,* vol. 6 (London: Darton, Longman & Todd, 1974), 390-398; Karl Rahner, "Atheism and Implicit Christianity," 145-164; "Anonymous Christianity and the Missionary Task of the Church," in *Theological Investigations,* vol. 12 (New York: The Seabury Press, 1974), 161-178; "Anonymous and Explicit Faith," in *Theological Investigations,* vol. 16 (New York: The Seabury Press, 1979), 52-59; "The One Christ, and the Universality of Salvation," in *Theological Investigations,* vol. 16, 199-224. The always insightful Avery Dulles observes that the notion of anonymous Christianity was quite common among modern (liberal) theologians, Avery Dulles, *The Dimensions of the Church: A Postconciliar Reflection* (Westminster, Maryland: Newman Press, 1966), 47: "Because of this real but unrecognized relationship to Christ as their Redeemer, modern theologians sometimes speak in this connection of 'latent' (Tillich) or 'anonymous' (Rahner) Christians or 'unconscious Christianity' (Bonhoeffer)."

[23]   Karl Rahner, "Atheism and Implicit Christianity," 145.

salvation for all.[24] So he says, "Christianity does not simply confront the member of an extra-Christian religion as a mere non-Christian but as someone who can and must already be regarded in this or that aspect as an anonymous Christian. It would be wrong to regard the pagan as someone who has not yet been touched in any way by God's grace and truth." There is something of an implicit faith (*fides implicita*) in them.[25]

As we noted, Rahner's theory is actually philosophical in nature. God's revelation is the "Absolute Being," or the Transcendent each person confronts during his cognitive reflections and during his experiences—this revelation is some "wordless interiority." In this encounter, God offers himself in grace and as the person responds truly and authentically, he is exercising a type of implicit faith. This experience will not emerge in explicit terms for those in other religions or for those who have rejected explicit Christianity, but their altruistic lives indicate that this grace has been accepted. The premise to his view is that all human spirits are oriented to God as the Absolute Being, and that God, being the horizon of all knowing and willing, communicates Himself continuously.[26] So, "God is the precondition which makes human spiritual experiences possible. God is not identical with me but is intimately present to me, giving me the ability to express—and thus to experience—my spirituality....When we are most aware of ourselves, we place ourselves most completely in the presence of God."[27] To be really human is to know God.[28] He has said elsewhere that "theology and anthropology necessarily become one."[29] In brief, that is Rahner's

---

[24]   This is summed up in Karl Rahner, "Christianity and the Non-Christian Religions," 115-134.
[25]   Ibid., 131.
[26]   For a more philosophical explanation, analysis, and critique, see J. A. DiNoia, "Implicit Faith, General Revelation and the State of Non-Christians," *The Thomist* 47 (1983): 209-241. His is not a Reformed assessment. A typical "Thomistic" critique of Thomistic Transcendentalism can be found in Robert J. Henle, "Transcendental Thomism, A Critical Assessment," in *One Hundred Years of Thomism: Aeterni Patris and Afterwards, A Symposium*, ed. Victor B. Brezik (Houston, TX: Center for Thomistic Studies, 1981), 90-116.
[27]   William A. Herr, *Catholic Thinkers in the Clear*, 254-55.
[28]   "The Concept of Mystery in Catholic Theology," in *Theological Investigations*, vol. 4 (1966; reprint, New York: The Seabury Press, 1974), 49: "We inquire therefore into man, as the being who is orientated to the mystery as such, this orientation being a constitutive element of his being both in his natural state and in his supernatural elevation."
[29]   Karl Rahner, *Foundations of Christian Faith: An Introduction to the Idea of Christianity*, trans. William V. Dych (New York: The Seabury Press, 1978), 44.

understanding. As speculative and radical as this is, it nonetheless radically influenced Catholicism.

We can best understand Rahner and Vatican II if we begin to grasp their view of revelation. Instead of viewing revelation in terms of special and general revelation, these thinkers began to view revelation in terms of God's self-communication that is proposition-less. Traditionally, most theologians recognized that non-Christian religions did not have God's special revelation, but modern Catholic (and many Protestant) theologians believe other religions and each human being have access to God's revelation which they believe may be sufficient. As one writer says, "Thus Catholic theologians no longer equate divine revelation solely with Holy Scripture or divine doctrine. The highly conceptual understanding of divine revelation has been superseded, and revelation is now understood as more than propositional truth. From the standpoint of the Christian faith, revelation is understood as a divine self-disclosure."[30] This means that God is revealing Himself to everyone—not as through general revelation—but secretly and sufficiently in and to each person. These modern Catholic theologians believe the act of self-communication itself is a gracious move on the part of God and can easily, if not inevitably, become salvific.

So what do we have? Protestants, other religions, and even atheists are *not* excluded. The Second Vatican Council wanted to revamp Catholicism and it did. Since this was an ecumenical council, the RC Church cannot minimize Vatican II's authoritative teaching. She must begin to embrace these liberalizing interpretations.

The Second Vatican documents rarely if ever closed the door tightly. It effectively broadened the Roman Catholic Church. Her outlook now is optimistic and liberal; she is less narrow and dogmatic. She praises more and condemns less; she embraces almost everyone and rejects few. This is how Rahner views the church two decades after the Second Vatican Council: "Formerly theology asked apprehensively, how man are saved from the *massa damnata* of world-history. Today we ask whether we may hope that all are saved."[31] In 1966, he had said something similar: The Christian "may not have as his own that idea of the early Christians that all the members of the Church are those who, by

---

[30]   Robert A. Burns, *Roman Catholicism after Vatican II*, 139.
[31]   K. Rahner, "The Abiding Significance of Vatican II," in *Theological Investigations: Concern for the Church*, trans. E. Quinn, vol. 20 (New York: Crossroad, 1981), 101.

and large, have been called out of the *massa damnata* of the rest of mankind unto salvation."[32] Other Catholic theologians support this assessment.[33] Even in 2001, one Roman Catholic scholar reflecting on the impact of the Second Vatican said, "Despite these objections and others that have been raised by well-respected theologians, the fact is that, apart from the questions of terminology such as anonymous Christianity and with differences of emphasis and detail, Rahner's position is undoubtedly the position of modern mainstream Catholic theology. The salvation optimism that Rahner has described is one of the most extraordinary developments in Catholic theology today."[34] In other words, what we have set forth is not peripheral to Catholicism. Some are convinced that it is *mainstream* Catholicism!

The Second Vatican changed Roman Catholicism. It was neither a renewal nor a reformation. It was a massive stab in the heart of her theology and it fundamentally changed the essence of that church. She swallowed a poisonous pill that has permanently crippled her. It may actually lead to her slow death. Reactions to this Council are varied, and their reactions will more or less determine if the Catholicism we know will continue or not. Her entire future depends on how she responds to the Second Vatican.

REACTIONS TO VATICAN II

Catholicism is not monolithic because she possesses within her walls all the extremes of Protestantism. Rome has their moderates, extreme liberals, as well as staunch conservatives. The entire Roman Catholic enterprise depends on how the different Popes interpret and incorporate Vatican II statements. If the Pope runs with the liberalizing

---

[32] K. Rahner, *The Church after the Council,* trans. D. C. Herron and R. Albrecht (New York: Herder & Herder, 1966), 52. Rahner is quite convinced that everything had changed in regard to the fate of those outside the church, see "What Does the Vatican II Teach about Atheism?," in *Concilium—Theology in the Age of Renewal,* ed. Karl Rahner, vol. 23 (New York: Paulist Press, 1967), 7-24.
[33] Richard P. McBrien, "The Church (*Lumen Gentium*)," in *Modern Catholicism: Vatican II and After* (New York: Oxford University Press, 1991), 90: "The human race is no longer seen as a *massa damnata* from whom a few are saved to manifest the glory and mercy of God, but as an essentially saved community from whom a few may, by the exercise of their own free will, be lost." Admittedly, in the whole Roman Catholic spectrum, McBrien represents the liberal wing of the church. Not all would agree with his assessment, but it seems fair enough, given the evidence offered here.
[34] Robert A. Burns, *Roman Catholicism after Vatican II* (Washington, D.C.: Georgetown University Press, 2001), 151.

spirit of Second Vatican, then Catholicism will go the way of all liberal denominations. If, on the other hand, the Pope narrows and mutes the voice of the Second Vatican, then she will forever have to explain how the *Magisterium* never erred.[35]

Joseph Ratzinger (when he was Joseph Cardinal Ratzinger, before becoming Pope Benedict XVI) said that the content of the Second Vatican "was entirely in keeping with the tradition of the Church."[36] He is being consistent with his Catholicism. He said, "It is likewise impossible to decide *in favor* of Trent and Vatican I, but *against* Vatican II. Whoever denies Vatican II denies the authority that upholds the other two councils and thereby detaches them from their foundation."[37] Ratzinger is convinced that Vatican II does not "rupture" the continuity but is in continuity with the entire church. For him, there is no pre- or post-conciliar church. "I should like to say that Vatican II surely did not want 'to change' the faith, but to represent it in a more effective way."[38] Pope Benedict, therefore, believes it is possible to embrace all the previous teachings, along with the declarations of the Second Vatican.

The previous Pope (John Paul II) was considered by many progressive Catholics to have been "traditional." Hastings believes that John Paul II may have effectively stifled the progress of Vatican II. He is convinced that Rome can only survive if she accedes to the Vatican II principle.[39] Yet John Paul II is not as traditional as Hastings made him out to be. John Paul II did much to advance the ecumenical dialogues with other religions. This could not have happened without Vatican II.

Karl Rahner, however, interpreted John Paul II differently from Hastings. In the early 1980s he penned these words:

---

[35] There are some who bemoan the fact that the changes envisaged by the Second Vatican have been arrested, see Hervé Legrand, "Forty Years Later: What has become of the Ecclesiological Reforms envisaged by Vatican II?," in *Concilium—Vatican II: A Forgotten Future?*, ed. Alberto Melloni and Christoph Theobald (London: SCM Press, 2005), 57-72.

[36] Joseph Cardinal Ratzinger, *Principles of Catholic Theology: Building Stones for a Fundamental Theology,* trans. Sister Mary Frances McCarthy, S.N.D. (San Francisco: Ignatius Press, 1987), 379.

[37] Joseph Ratzinger and Vittorio Messori, *The Ratzinger Report: An Exclusive Interview on the State of the Church,* trans. Salvator Attanasio and Graham Harrison (San Francisco: Ignatius Press, 1986), 28.

[38] Ibid., 35.

[39] A. Hastings, "Catholic History from Vatican I to John Paul II," in *Modern Catholicism: Vatican II and After*, 8-13

The Pope embraces non-Catholic church leaders and pagans; a Roman cardinal declared in Tunis that Mohammed had been a true prophet; all ecumenical conversations assume that all the partners to the discussion are living in the grace of God. Although rejecting theoretical doctrine of universal reconciliation, the Church in the Council and in its practical conduct starts out from the assumption that God's grace is not only offered to man's free decision, but also that it largely prevails universally in this freedom. This attitude of the Church came into existence of course only after a very long period of development. But it became clear and irreversible in the Second Vatican Council; for such a hope can certainly grow, while it can no longer really decline.[40]

His statement is very accurate. The "irreversible" effects of the Second Vatican Council have raised their ugly heads. Most secular newscasters and talking heads view the Pope as being conservative (and on moral issues he is), but they are not the best judges of his theological teachings.

In 1964, during the Second Vatican Council, Pope Paul VI set up a Council to facilitate dialogue with other religions which is now called "Pontifical Council for Interreligious Dialogue."[41] Though none of us would deny the importance of speaking with other religions, the council (PCID) praises them almost as brothers.[42] Pope John Paul II (Karol Wojtyla, 1978-2005) spoke with great deference for the Second Vatican Council's teaching on non-Christian religions in his encyclical *Redemptor Hominis*. He said (in concert with the Second Vatican) that all "the various religions ... [are] many reflections of the one truth."[43] There is also the mystical universalistic language of Rahner and Vatican II in Pope John Paul II when he speculates about the incarnation and the destiny of humanity; namely, somehow, the mere fact of incarnation has

---

[40]   K. Rahner, "The Abiding Significance of Vatican II," 101.
[41]   The official Vatican account: "On Pentecost Sunday, 1964, Pope Paul VI instituted a special department of the Roman Curia for relations with the people of other religions. Known at first as the Secretariat for Non Christians, in 1988 it was renamed the Pontifical Council for Interreligious Dialogue (PCID)." See http://www.vatican.va/roman_curia/pontifical_councils/interelg/documents/rc_pc_interel g_pro_20051996_en.html
[42]   See the site http://www.vatican.va/roman_curia/pontifical_councils/interelg/index.htm.
[43]   Claudia Carlen Ihm, ed., "Redemptor Hominis," in *The Papal Encyclicals*, 5 vols. (Wilmington, NC: McGrath, 1981), 5:252 (§ 29).

affected all of humanity— "Christ 'united himself with each man.'"[44]
The Roman Curia under Pope John Paul II also spoke of the good in all
religions.[45]

Pope Benedict XVI may be attempting to change the trend (see
his "Message of His Holiness Benedict XVI to Bishop Domenico
Sorrentino on the occasion of the 20th Anniversary of the Interreligious
Meeting of Prayer for Peace" delivered on Oct. 27, 2006). He is careful
to avoid what some had perceived to be religious relativism in Pope John
Paul II.[46] He may in fact be more conservative than Pope John Paul II.[47]
Benedict XVI demoted Archbishop Fitzgerald because he disagreed with
Fitzgerald's dialogue with other religions. Pope Benedict is at least more
conservative than the Archbishop on the matter of religious relativism.[48]
It still remains to be seen at this point in history where he will take the

---

[44] *Redemptor Hominis*, 262 (§ 68-69). Pope John Paul II was in fact quoting Vatican II.

[45] "The Council proceeds further. Making its own the vision and the terminology of some early Church Fathers, Nostra Aetate speaks of the presence in these traditions of "a ray of that Truth which enlightens all" (NA 2). Ad Gentes recognizes the presence of "seeds of the word", and points to "the riches which a generous God has distributed among the nations" (AG 11). Again, Lumen Gentium refers to the good which is "found sown" not only "in minds and hearts", but also "in the rites and customs of peoples" (LG 17)." This is from "PONTIFICAL COUNCIL FOR INTER-RELIGIOUS DIALOGUE/DIALOGUE AND PROCLAMATION/Reflection And Orientations On Interreligious Dialogue And The Proclamation Of The Gospel Of Jesus Christ" which is found http://www.vatican.va/roman_curia/pontifical_councils/interelg/documents/rc_pc_interel g_doc_19051991_dialogue-and-proclamatio_en.html .

[46] This can be seen in his message to Bishop Domenico Sorrentino. See http://www.vatican.va/holy_father/benedict_xvi/letters/2006/documents/hf_ben-xvi_let_20060902_xx-incontro-assisi_en.html.

[47] Avery Dulles placed Ratzinger (among the several factions within the Synod) into the more conservative group which he called "Neo-Augustinians" during the Extraordinary Synod of 1985. See Avery Dulles, *The Reshaping of Catholicism: Current Challenges in the Theology of Church* (San Francisco: Harper & Row, 1988), 191. However, earlier in his career, Ratzinger sounded like a neo-orthodox theologian of the Barthian strain. In Karl Rahner and Joseph Ratzinger, *Revelation and Tradition,* trans. W. J. O'Hara (New York: Herder and Herder, 1966), 35-37, he says, "It might also be said that scripture is the material principle of revelation…but that it is not revelation itself…For revelation always and only becomes a reality where there is faith…Consequently revelation to some degree includes its recipient, without whom it does not exist. Revelation cannot be pocketed like a book one carries around…Scripture *is* not revelation but at most only a part of the latter's great reality."

[48] http://www.ad2000.com.au/articles/2006/apr2006p2_2198.html .

MARK A. HERZER   89

Roman Catholic institution. Nonetheless, this strong ecumenical tendency has not disappeared.

We've cited these things to demonstrate that Vatican II lives on and must live on if Roman Catholicism wishes to be true to her understanding of tradition and the *Magisterium*. So devastating and extensive *is* the influence of the Second Vatican that some have vigorously fought the liberalizing trend. The most popular example is Archbishop Lefebvre, who courageously resisted it and was eventually excommunicated (on June 30, 1988 when he ordained four bishops).[49] He said in 1974, "We refuse, on the other hand, and have always refused to follow the Rome of neo-Modernist and neo-Protestant tendencies which were clearly evident in the Second Vatican Council and, after the Council, in all the reforms which issued from it."[50] He believed that the Council was "entirely corrupt" and condemned the ecumenical dialogues with the heretical Protestants. He spoke as a true traditionalist (following the influence of the Integralists)[51] and continued to use the Tridentine Mass (remember, the liturgy of the Mass changed).[52]   An ultra conservative dissident group elected another Pope and is waiting for the day when it can take over the Vatican.[53] They believe that the Second Vatican Council is heretical and that the church has been without a pope

---

[49]   W. D. Dinges, "Lefebvre, Marcel," in *The New Catholic Encyclopedia*, ed. Berard L. Marthaler, 2nd ed., 15 vols. (Washington, D.C.: Gale in association with The Catholic University of America, 2003), 8:446-449; W. D. Dinges, *Roman Catholic Traditionalism,* ed. M. E. Marty and R. S. Appleby, Fundamentalisms Observed, vol. 1 (Chicago: The University of Chicago Press, 1991), 66-141; Michael J. Walsh, "The Conservative Reaction," in *Modern Catholicism: Vatican II and After*, 283-288.
[50]   See http://www.geocities.com/SSPXCath/1974.html .
[51]   Integralism was a campaign against modernism by the Roman curial officials. This movement was given a permanent position by Pius X through his encyclical *Pascendi* (1907). Traditionalists after Vatican II maintained the spirit of integralism. Not surprisingly, Lefebvre started the Society of St. Pius X (SSPX) to propagate traditionalism. See "Integralism" in *New Catholic Encyclopedia*, 7:503-504 and W. Dinges, "Roman Catholic Traditionalism," 78-83. For an historical account, see Gabriel Daly, *Transcendence and Immanence: A Study in Catholic Modernism and Integralism* (Oxford: Clarendon Press, 1980) and Darrell Jodock, ed., *Catholicism Contending with Modernity: Roman Catholic and Anti-Modernism in Historical Context* (Cambridge: Cambridge University Press, 2000), 82-86.
[52]   Once the *Novus Ordo* Mass was implemented, it coexisted with the Tridentine for a few years (April 1969 to Nov. 1971). In 1971, the celebration of the Tridentine Mass was prohibited. However, in 2007, the Latin Mass was once again permitted to co-exist with the vernacular.
[53]   It is difficult to ascertain the history of this group. I cannot be certain how much (if any) Lefebvre influenced this group.

for about forty years (until they voted in a new one).[54] This, no doubt, is a very fringe group. Nevertheless, most traditionalists still reject large parts of the Second Vatican Council.[55]

So Roman Catholicism is not "healthy." She is a different opponent and we must take that into account in our polemics against her. Unfortunately, many good critiques against Catholicism do not sufficiently address this modern liberalizing trend.[56] Every assessment of Roman Catholicism must consider the damage caused by the Second Vatican. But at the same time, we must not think that everything has changed. Even with all the liberalizing tendencies in her, she still holds many of the older and problematic doctrines. These heresies have not disappeared; they still permeate their dogmas. Those dogmas continue to remain as enduring obstacles to any genuine fellowship with Rome.

CATHOLIC ECUMENISM & MODERN EVANGELICALS

As we all know, many Evangelicals have made great efforts to bring about some rapprochement between Protestants and Catholics. In 1994, *First Things* published their "Evangelicals and Catholics Together."[57] Over the years, they have issued four statements, the last one in 2003.[58] The dialogue has been reflective and illuminating at some points. Many Evangelicals protested and were rightly suspicious of the efforts. After all this, one wonders what really has been accomplished.

Most recently, Mark Noll's and Carolyn Nystrom's book *Is the Reformation Over?* also strongly encouraged a union but with some caveats.[59] This well researched book is very disappointing because it leans towards the virtues of Catholicism and tends to maximize the

---

[54]   See http://www.truecatholic.org/ .
[55]   See http://en.wikipedia.org/wiki/Traditionalist_Catholicism .
[56]   Two good works can be cited, James R. White, *The Roman Catholic Controversy* (Minneapolis: Bethany House Publishers, 1996) and William Webster, *The Church of Rome at the Bar of History* (Carlisle, PA: The Banner of Truth Trust, 1995). These are fine works and I do not wish to diminish the benefits of their polemical efforts.
[57]   "The Christian Mission in the Third Millenium," *First Things* (May 1994): 15-21.
[58]   "The Communion of Saints," *First Things* (March 2003): 26-33. ECT II can be found in "The Gift of Salvation," *Christianity Today*, December 8, 1997, 35-37; ECT III, "Your Word is Truth" in *Your Word is Truth*, ed. Charles Colson and Richard John Neuhaus (Grand Rapids: Eerdmans, 2002), 1-8. All four statements can be found on the internet site of *First Things*.
[59]   Mark Noll and Carolyn Nystrom, *Is the Reformation Over? An Evangelical Assessment of Contemporary Roman Catholicism* (Grand Rapids: Baker, 2005).

weaknesses in evangelicalism.[60] For example, ample attention is given to converts to Catholicism while no examples of the reverse were cited. They admit this, but give no real reason for their lack of balance.[61] Noll and Nystrom seem to reduce the whole debate to ecclesiology and language differences. They do not adequately and carefully deal with theological differences. While some broad differences are noted, the more technical differences are overlooked. The authors frequently suggest that many good things dominate Catholicism and that Catholics and Protestants have much in common theologically. But they failed to observe that those common things have always existed since the reformation (Trinity, Ecumenical Creeds, etc.). Those common things were insufficient for the Reformers.

Catholics have been very busy dialoguing with various protestant denominations. Anglicans, Methodists, Pentecostals, Reformed, Lutherans, Disciples of Christ, Baptists, and Evangelicals have all been involved in these massive efforts.[62] Mark Noll's assessment of the whole well summarizes the effects of this endeavor: "On the basis of the ecumenical dialogues, can it be said that the Reformation is over? Probably not. But a once-yawning chasm has certainly narrowed."[63] But what has been achieved? Some Catholic scholars are disappointed because these enterprises look more like "the management of present diversities than like a rapid process of unification among the Churches."[64]

In the end, I believe, all these efforts do not take seriously the liberalism which plagues modern Catholicism. The attempt to unite and

---

[60] I think the best review on this book is James R. White, review of *Is the Reformation Over?* by Mark A. Noll and Carolyn Nystrom, *Reformed Baptist Theological Review* 3, no. 2 (July 2006): 141-145.

[61] Noll, *Is the Reformation Over?*, 200-207. "This chapter treated only evangelical to Catholic conversions. Were it a different book, it would be important to hear from the many who converted from Catholicism to various branches of Protestantism," (207).

[62] The reports and conclusions have been compiled in Harding Meyer and Lucas Vischer, ed., *Growth in Agreement: Reports and Agreed Statements of Ecumenical Conversation on a World Level* (New York: Paulist Press, 1984); Jeffrey Gros, Harding Meyer and William G. Rusch, ed., *Growth in Agreement, II: Reports and Agreed Statements of Ecumenical Conversations on a World Level, 1982-1998* (Grand Rapids: Eerdmans, 2000). A good overview of these massive two volumes can be found in Noll's *Is the Reformation Over*, 75-114.

[63] Noll, *Is the Reformation Over?*, 114.

[64] Alberto Melloni and Christoph Theobald, ed., *Vatican II: A Forgotten Future?* (London: SCM Press, 2005), 39.

dialogue is part of the Second Vatican agenda. Though the post-Vatican II church moved further away from its historic position, it has not discarded many of the key doctrines that have compelled the Reformation. In a sense, any dialogue with Catholicism is suspect because we cannot be certain if they are taking doctrinal convictions seriously. At times, ecumenism seems to be the only stable spirit in Catholicism. In addition, a post Vatican II church is dialoging with a confused form of Protestantism.[65] Fuzzy minded evangelicals are hardly in a position to dialogue with fickle minded Catholics. Protestants seem to have given up on doctrinal clarity and faithfulness while many Catholics have embraced the confused faithlessness of liberal scholarship. Darryl Hart's cynical observation is worth quoting: "...instead of asking, 'Is the Reformation over?' perhaps a better question to ask is whether evangelicalism is finished."[66]

Noll and Nystrom do make a passing reference to some Catholics who reject Vatican II, but they never give it any analysis.[67] This dissent within Catholicism suggests that something more has happened to Catholicism than simply that she is more congenial to Protestantism. The Catholicism we are dealing with now has been forever marked by the Second Vatican. We are not dealing with a chaste, open Catholicism but one which is struggling with liberalism, and it remains to be seen which way she will go. To speak of unity with Catholicism is in the least premature because the poisonous effects of Vatican II are still manipulating her identity.

Furthermore, Catholic ecumenical endeavors are simply the agenda set by the Second Vatican. In other words, this effort on their part is programmatic of their new way of looking at life. Dulles says, "Vatican II formally committed the Catholic church to the ideals and goals of ecumenism." In fact, the Extraordinary Synod of 1985 reaffirmed the spirit of Vatican II by stating "ecumenism has inscribed itself deeply and indelibly in the consciousness of the Church."[68] Rather than just accepting this, we should ask, "Why should we dialogue? If there is such freedom in accepting other religions, should we not be

---

[65]   See Darryl Hart, *Deconstructing Evangelicalism: Conservative Protestantism in the Age of Billy Graham* (Grand Rapids: Baker Books, 2004).

[66]   D. G. Hart, "Does Protestantism Have What Evangelicals are Looking For?," *Modern Reformation* 14, no.5 (September/October 2005): 24.

[67]   Noll, *Is the Reformation Over?*, 230.

[68]   Avery Dulles, *The Reshaping of Catholicism: Current Challenges in the Theology of Church* (San Francisco: Harper & Row, 1988), 227.

suspicious of where this ecumenical spirit is coming from and to where it will lead?"

One thing that everyone fails to mention is that we do not have the kind of dogmatic treatises that used to mark Catholicism. Where are their Otts, Tanquereys, Pohle & Preusses, Hunters, and the like? Though we may seriously disagree with their theology, we knew where they stood. Modern Catholic theologians are more speculative, philosophical, and non-committal. The works of Keating, Hahn, and Sungenis lack the depth and learning of their previous forefathers. The modern works of Rahner[69] and O'Collins[70] are heavily philosophical and skeptical in nature. If these works are a foretaste of what we can expect from Catholic scholarship, then any discussion of "Evangelicals and Catholics Together" is inane. It is akin to the Presbyterian Church in America entertaining a merger with the Presbyterian Church USA (PCUSA). No trend or change in the PCUSA indicates that she is moving in the right direction. To dialogue with Catholicism will be as fruitful as dialoging with the PCUSA.

Noll and Nystrom have also failed to take into the account the incredible resurgence of Catholic apologetics. This strong apologetic effort to convert Protestants to Catholicism blankets the airwaves. This form of invigorated Catholicism is filled with Protestant defectors. EWTN, through its Television and Radio ministry, has put a clean conservative edge to Catholicism.[71] *Catholic Answers*, Karl Keating, Scott Hahn, *The Coming Home Network International*, and similar voices do not exist to dialogue. These Catholics are attempting to convert Protestants to Catholicism. Noll and Nystrom never suggest that such efforts even exist. The irenic picture of Catholicism does not do justice to modern Catholicism in America.

WHAT HAS NOT CHANGED

Having argued that Catholicism has fundamentally changed, I am not suggesting that everything is different. Many of their doctrinal formulations still stand. There are several key doctrines that will always

---

[69]   His massive 23 volume work entitled *Theological Investigations*.
[70]   Gerald O'Collins, *Fundamental Theology* (New York: Paulist Press, 1981).
[71]   EWTN means "Eternal Word Television Network" (EWTN Global Catholic Network). It began in 1981.

keep us apart unless they change their position.[72] The only way for Catholics and Protestants to unite is to *minimize* the doctrinal differences and overlook them as being non-essential. For example, the prolific and often insightful Roman Catholic Cardinal Avery Dulles suggested the following as one of the ways of coming into fellowship with each other: "the different churches can come into closer communion if they recognize that one another's binding doctrines are, if not true, at least not manifestly repugnant to the revelation given in Christ."[73] In other words, if we concede that the other view is not "repugnant" to what God's Word teaches, then we can come into closer communion with them. That is *not* a viable option.

DOCTRINAL DEVELOPMENT

Before addressing *some* of the key doctrines that thwart fellowship, a word needs to be said about their view of doctrine and doctrinal developments. More and more Catholics are reticent about the binding nature of all of the church's teaching. In Vatican I, the Pope declared that his *ex cathedra* statements are "irreformable" (irreformabiles).[74] That position has been maintained up to the Second Vatican.[75] In Vatican II, they softened this doctrine (*UR* 17): "It is hardly surprising, then, if from time to time one tradition has come nearer to a full appreciation of some aspects of a mystery of revelation than the other, or has expressed it to better advantage." Similar concepts can be found in *Gaudiem et Spes*.[76] The older Vatican I understanding of unchanging dogmas and traditions has been roundly criticized.[77]

Moderates like Avery Dulles argue that our "sociocultural factors" must be considered. We must "reckon with the historical

---

[72]   For a brief but helpful reason why we must continue to resist Catholicism, see Michael Horton, "Can We Be Confessional and Catholic? Prospects of Christian Unity Today," *Modern Reformation* 14, no. 5 (September/October 2005): 9-18.

[73]   Avery Dulles, *The Reshaping of Catholicism: Current Challenges in the Theology of Church,* 236.

[74]   *Pastor Aeternus,* First dogmatic constitution on the church of Christ, §4.

[75]   The Modernists were roundly condemned all the way up to Vatican II. See my footnote above on Integralism. See a good overview in Avery Dulles, *The Survival of Dogma* (Garden City, NY: Doubleday & Company, Inc., 1971), 185-189.

[76]   See the references in Avery Dulles, *The Survival of Dogma,* 189-190.

[77]   Once again Archbishop Cardinal Lefebvre represents that small dying wing; See Dulles, *The Reshaping Catholicism,* 78.

conditioning of all ecclesiastical statements."[78] He believes that "all doctrinal formulations are inadequate."[79] Every theological statement has "an element of provisionality" and every dogmatic definition is "not so much an end as a beginning."[80] This sounds very much like post-modernism before its time. He develops this a bit more in another book. Tradition, for Dulles, is something like an intuitive or experiential knowledge that must be handed down from generation to generation. It is more than mere dogma; it is a living experience.[81]

What does all this mean? In the worst sense, it means that each generation has to affirm what it believes in its own way. What was meaningful back then may no longer mean the same thing now. They would argue that some doctrines simply no longer have prominence the way they did before. Another way of interpreting this (using Dulles's way of always turning a positive spin) is to simply recognize we don't all have the truth.

Their view of doctrinal development means things are not as they seem. If socio-cultural and linguistic contexts are carefully considered, then seemingly contradictory statements may actually coexist. Dulles gives an example that may surprise us. "Thus a Catholic of the sixteenth century, giving a certain understanding to the term 'faith,' might deny that man was saved by faith alone. Today, with a wider understanding of the same term, he might affirm the proposition then denied. The two statements would not be really contradictory, for the meaning of one of the terms would have been changed."[82] This explains why modern Catholic theologians can both embrace the

---

[78]   Avery Dulles, *The Survival of Dogma*, 182. Neo-orthodox statements can be found in this work on the same page.
[79]   Ibid., 183.
[80]   Ibid., 196-197. The latter phrase is taken from Rahner, "Current Problems in Christology," *Theological Investigations*, vol. 1 (Baltimore: Helicon Press, 1961), 159-50. This same theme is repeated nearly twenty years later in Dulles's *The Reshaping of Catholicism*, 88.
[81]   In *The Reshaping of Catholicism*, 86, Avery Dulles says, "I conclude, then, that the essential and primary function of Christian tradition is not to transmit explicit knowledge, which can better be done by written documents, nor simply to provide a method of discovery, but to impart a tacit, lived awareness of the God to whom the Christian Scriptures and symbols point."
[82]   Dulles, *The Survival of Dogma*, 199-200. His more developed view of justification by faith can be found in Avery Dulles, "A Roman Catholic View of Justification in light of the Dialogues," in *By Faith Alone: Essays on Justification in Honor of Gerhard O. Forde*, ed. Joseph A. Burgess and Mark Kolden (Grand Rapids: William B Eerdmans Publications Company, 2004), 220-231.

Tridentine formulas and anathemas and enter into dialogue with evangelicals. They believe Vatican II is the innovative overflow of their view of tradition. They see no problem in affirming two seemingly contradictory statements because they were formulated in two different eras. So, when we deal with the following specific doctrines, their view of doctrinal progress must be taken into account.

SOLA SCRIPTURA

It has been traditionally argued that the Council of Trent taught a theory of two-source authority, namely, scripture and tradition.[83] Some argue that this has been a great misunderstanding.[84] Catholics, they say, believe in the primacy of Scripture, and tradition plays a role in determining its meaning. This novel and controversial position did not hold much sway.[85] If this position was as certain as Geiselmann and others had made it out to be, then there would be room for "dialog" with Roman Catholics.[86] But the Vatican II documents state emphatically that "the church's certainty about all that is revealed is not drawn from holy scripture alone; both scripture and tradition are to be accepted and

---

[83]   The Council of Trent said that the truth is "contained in the written books and in the unwritten traditions, which have been received by the apostles from the mouth of Christ Himself, or from the apostles themselves at the dictation of the Holy Spirit, (and has) come down even to us, transmitted as it were from hand to hand" (Denzinger, 783, cited in Berkouwer, *The Second Vatican Council and the New Catholicism*, 92).

[84]   It had originally read, "partly Scripture…partly tradition" (partim…partim) on April 1, 1546 and then on April 8 it finally read "Scripture and tradition" (literally, "in written books and in unwritten traditions," i.e., *in libris scriptis et sine scripto traditionibus*). See Berkouwer, *The Second Vatican Council and the New Catholicism*, trans. Lewis B. Smedes (Grand Rapids: Eerdmans, 1965), 95; S. Ferguson, "Scripture and Tradition," in *Sola Scriptura: The Protestant Position on the Bible*, ed. D. Kistler (Morgan, PA: Soli Deo Gloria, 1995), 212-213; and especially, J. R. Geiselmann, "Scripture, Tradition, and the Church: An Ecumenical Problem," in *Christianity Divided: Protestant and Roman Catholic Theological Issues*, ed. D. J. Callahan, H. A. Oberman and D. J. O'Hanlon (New York: Sheed and Ward, 1961), 39-50. Also see Robert B. Strimple, "The Relationship between Scripture and Tradition in Contemporary Roman Catholic Theology," *Westminster Theological Journal* 40 (Fall 1977): 22-38.

[85]   Sinclair Ferguson gives a good overview and response in his "Scripture and Tradition," 214ff.

[86]   Robert Strimple has shown that Geiselmann did not believe that Scripture itself was normative; both Scripture and tradition served as a kerygma – not infallible sources. Strimple calls him post-Bultmannian. See Strimple, "The Relationship between Scripture and Tradition in Contemporary Roman Catholic Theology," 1-32.

honoured with like devotion and reverence" (*DV* 9).[87] The Council of Trent, Vatican II, and *The Catechism of the Catholic Church* (§ 76-79) all teach a dual source of authority.

Some Catholics believe that Vatican II allowed for a new way of approaching tradition. "Tradition" is defined not as propositions but as "a process of transmission." Vatican II, they say, taught that tradition is "the practice and life of the believing and praying Church."[88] Lest you misunderstand what is being said here, let me explain. They are saying that tradition cannot bear revelation if people do not believe. Only when they believe is there a living tradition: "If there were no community of believers, revelation as a transaction would be cut short."[89] Put simply, rather than viewing tradition as an extra source of revelation on par with Scripture, you should view it as a living community that embraces revelation. This somehow, it is believed, will enable Protestants and Catholics to come together.

Before we criticize, it must be noted that Catholics do not believe that there are two sources of revelation. They never say that tradition is the Word of God. Scripture is the Word of God (*DV* 24).[90] Protestants have recognized this. Bavinck argues that the Roman Catholic church "has not yet progressed to the point where it dares to equate ecclesiastical interpretation with divine truth."[91] The same has been noted by Strimple, "Ecclesiastical tradition has never been considered by the Roman Church to be revelation."[92] What is the relationship? One of their writers gives a good distinction: "Thus there is a sense in which Catholics, as well as Protestants, can speak of Scripture as being finally normative. But while tradition cannot contradict the true meaning of Scripture, Scripture cannot be confidently identified or authoritatively interpreted without the help of tradition."[93] What they

---

[87] In *DV* 7, they utilize the phrase "sacred tradition and the sacred scripture of the two testaments."
[88] Avery Dulles, *Models of Revelation* (Garden City, NY: Doubleday & Company, Inc., 1983), 223.
[89] Ibid., 220.
[90] See Avery Dulles, "Revelation, Fonts of," in *The New Catholic Encyclopedia*, ed. Berard L. Marthaler, 2nd ed., vol. 12 (Washington, D.C.: Gale in association with The Catholic University of America, 2003), 190-193.
[91] Herman Bavinck, *Reformed Dogmatics,* trans. John Vriend, vol. 1 (Grand Rapids: Baker Academic, 2003), 118.
[92] Strimple, "The Relationship between Scripture and Tradition in Contemporary Roman Catholic Theology," 23.
[93] Dulles, "Revelation, Fonts of," 192.

concede on one hand, they take away with the other. Let me illustrate the absurdity of this position. It is like a young boy saying, "O.K., my parents have authority over me and what they say I must do. But, I can never know *who* my parents are and *what* they are really saying until my next door neighbor tells me. If they tell me, then I will obey my parents." What this young boy affirmed initially has been undone by appealing to another authority.

Protestants cannot accept their dual source of authority. *Sola Scriptura* must be the *principium* of all our theology. The Word gave life to the Church and the Word gives life to the church; without the Word, there is no church and the church cannot go on without the Word. The church did not create the word but merely recognized it; the Word does not need the church, while the church cannot exist without the Word.

JUSTIFICATION

The doctrine of justification is being undermined by the "New Perspective" on Paul and the Ecumenical enterprise of the Roman Catholic Church.[94] This doctrine alone makes any sort of union with Catholicism an impossible task. Until Rome comes to a true and Protestant understanding of Justification by Faith *alone*, we cannot unite.

As we know, the Council of Trent condemned Protestants and has categorically opposed the Protestant view (many of the thirty-three canons on Justification).[95] Vatican II did not do anything to change this. The new 1994 *The Catechism of the Catholic Church* also did not change this. The noted Catholic theologian Avery Dulles admits along with the Lutherans that the declarative aspect of justification is absent in the recent Catechism. He says, "The book does not seek to break new theological ground but to restate Catholic doctrine as already developed. The treatment of justification adheres closely to the teaching of the Council of Trent...."[96]

Trent viewed justification in terms of transformation. Justification is something that is done *in* us and not something done *for*

---

[94]   Michael Horton, "What's All the Fuss About? The Status of the Justification Debate," *Modern Reformation* 11, no. 2 (March/April 2002): 17-21.
[95]   Denzinger, *Enchiridion*, §1551-1583, or, the English translation, *Sources of Catholic Dogma*, §811-843.
[96]   Avery Dulles, "A Roman Catholic View of Justification in light of the Dialogues," in *By Faith Alone: Essays on Justification in Honor of Gerhard O. Forde*, ed. Joseph A. Burgess and Mark Kolden (Grand Rapids: William B Eerdmans Publications Company, 2004), 226.

us. Justification "consists not only in the forgiveness of sins but also in the sanctification and renewal of the inward being...." and this justification "makes us just (*nos iustus facit*)"(session 6, ch. 7).[97] Justification is also a process and something that increases "by faith united to good works (*cooperante fide bonis operibus* or "by faith cooperating with good works")" (ch. 10). They do admit that we are justified by faith and that faith is a gift (*gratis*) (ch. 8). Yet, this righteousness is something we have to preserve in us (since it is infused, *infusa*) "so that they may carry it before the tribunal of our lord Jesus Christ and possess eternal life." (ch. 7).

Vatican I and II did not change any of this.[98] The Catechism merely reaffirmed some of the statements from Trent.[99] It also states emphatically that "we can then merit for ourselves and for others the graces needed for our sanctification, for the increase of grace and charity, and for the attainment of eternal life."[100] Justification "includes...the renewal of the inner man."[101] Nothing has changed.

Ecumenical dialogues with Protestants have not brought any solutions. Noll's and Nystrom's attempt to put a positive spin to this, but admit that we will be disappointed. Then they add, "It is unlikely that any group of Catholics and evangelicals will come up with a united statement of forensic justification."[102] Even the declarations between Catholics and Lutherans failed (*Justification by Faith* and *Joint Declaration*). They came to a consensus, but not because they all came to terms with the Biblical view but rather because they all desired unity. Robert Preus, a noted Lutheran scholar, rightly pointed out that the climate has changed and that unity or consensus has been the driving force.[103] He says the controversy has not been settled "at least not in the sense of unequivocal meanings being attached to the key words making

[97] Tanner, *Decrees of the Ecumenical Council*, 2:673.
[98] This is also noted in "Justification," in *The New Catholic Encyclopedia*, 8:90 and in the ecumenical dialogue between Catholics and Lutherans, see H. George Anderson, T. Austin Murphy and Joseph A. Burgess, ed., *Justification by Faith: Lutherans and Catholics in Dialogue VII* (Minneapolis: Augsburg Publishing House, 1985), 41 (§73).
[99] See *Catechism of the Catholic Church*, §1987-1995.
[100] *Catechism of the Catholic Church*, §2010.
[101] Ibid.,§2019.
[102] Noll and Nystrom, *Is the Reformation Over?*, 180.
[103] Robert Preus, *Justification and Rome* (St. Louis: Concordia Academic Press, 1997), 106.

up the doctrine of justification."[104] He also notes that this document has been approved by the "Pontifical Council for Promoting Christian Unity" and not by the "Sacred Congregation for the Doctrine of the Faith."[105] The latter binds the Roman Catholic Church; the former does not. "The Joint Declaration, then, will have no effect whatsoever upon Rome's official doctrine at any point. Both the decrees and canons of the Council of Trent will remain fully intact and represent Rome's doctrinal position on the doctrine of justification, even if the canons are no longer activated....."[106] The ecumenical Roman Catholic theologian George Tavard admits as much, though he seems to be optimistic.[107]

For all the development in Catholicism and for all her changes, she has not changed Trent; she cannot change Trent.[108] The only thing they could say regarding the condemnations is that they no longer apply to the parties involved in the ecumenical dialogue or to "the teaching of the Lutheran churches presented in this declaration."[109] In other words, if we agree with those documents, we are not under the condemnations, but as the *Joint Declaration* itself states: "Nothing is thereby taken away from the seriousness of the condemnations related to the doctrine of justification, (§42)." The consensus statement is not completely forensic (§27 comes very close to it) nor is it *sola fide*. They can all say "By grace alone, in faith in Christ's saving work...." (§15) but notice, no *sola*

---

[104]   Ibid., 111.

[105]   Ibid., 112.

[106]   Ibid., 113.

[107]   George H. Tavard, "Overcoming the Anathemas: A Catholic View," in *By Faith Alone: Essays on Justification in Honor of Gerhard O. Forde*, 164-166.

[108]   Though language of *simul iustus et peccator* (at once righteous and sinful) can be found in *LG* 8 ("the church, containing sinners in its own bosom, is at one and the same time holy and always in need of purification and it pursues unceasingly penance and renewal"), it has not modified their view of justification sufficiently enough. Most of the astute Catholic theologians recognize this. For more on their struggle with this see Avery Dulles, *The Dimensions of the Church: A Postconciliar Reflection* (Westminster, Maryland: Newman Press, 1966), 29; "Justification in Contemporary Catholic Theology," in *Justification by Faith: Lutherans and Catholics in Dialogue VII*, 269-270.

[109]   See Karl Lehmann and Wolfhart Pannenberg, ed., *The Condemnations of the Reformation Era: Do They Still Divide?* (Minneapolis: Fortress Press, 1990); "Justification," in *New Catholic Encyclopedia*, 8:91; Jeffrey Gros, Harding Meyer and William G. Rusch, ed., *Growth in Agreement, II: Reports and Agreed Statements of Ecumenical Conversations on a World Level, 1982-1998* (Grand Rapids: Eerdmans, 2000), 573 (§41): "The teaching of the Lutheran churches presented in this declaration does not fall under the condemnations form the Council of Trent. The condemnations in the Lutheran confessions do not apply to the teaching of the Roman Catholic Church presented in this declaration."

fide![110] The *Joint Declaration* said nothing different than what the Council of Trent had already said (except that it was more irenic).

For this reason we cannot consider uniting with Catholicism—justification gets at the heart of the gospel. The consensus statements mask the differences. It is like a couple struggling in their marriage; it is falling apart—they have deep fundamental problems. To make their marriage work, they both throw themselves into a common hobby of stamp collecting. Yes, there might be some commonality and unity in their marriage, but the heart of the matter has never been touched or addressed. That analogy follows here. When all is said and done, *sola fide* has been skirted.

We must add that ECT II ("The Gift of Salvation") does use *sola fide* and its statement actually seems to be on the right track, but not completely. ECT II says that their statement "is in agreement with what the Reformation traditions have meant by justification by faith alone (*sola fide*)." However, it does not clearly state the reformation view of justification by faith alone. It does not state that we are justified by faith alone but only what they affirm agrees with what is meant by justification by faith alone. It is like a wife saying, "Honey, when I say 'I like you' you can take it to mean that it is in agreement with 'I love you.'" Would not her refusal to clearly declare her love be disturbing? Of course! Why can't Rome affirm boldly and unequivocally that we are justified by faith alone?

The problem with this unified statement is that the group does not have any official support from Rome. Timothy George, one of the signers, said that "this statement is not the result of an officially sponsored dialogue, but the collaborative work of individuals who speak from and to, but not for, our several communities."[111]

All these ecumenical attempts, once again, dodge this most important doctrine. Remember, Rome never denied we were justified by faith. But faith was never the *sufficient* condition for Rome. Reformers argued that we are justified by faith, by faith *alone*. Rome agreed we

---

[110] The Catholic Avery Dulles cannot seem to overcome *sola fide*; he seems reticent and at times has defined it away to maintain a Catholic position, see "Justification in Contemporary Catholic Theology," in *Justification by Faith: Lutherans and Catholics in Dialogue VII*, 265-266. He questions if it can really be found in Catholicism, see, "A Roman Catholic View of Justification in light of the Dialogues," in *By Faith Alone: Essays on Justification in Honor of Gerhard O. Forde*, 222.

[111] Timothy George, "An Evangelical Assessment," *Christianity Today* (December 8 1997): 34.

were justified by faith but not by faith alone. That a man could be immediately justified by faith is something more than a mere quibble over words. It gets at the heart of Roman Catholic theology and system. Bruce McCormack put it marvelously, "For the idea of an *immediate* divine imputation renders superfluous the entire Catholic system of the priestly mediation of grace by the Church."[112] In other words, since *sola fide* brings about immediate divine imputation, the doctrine would destroy Roman Catholicism root and branch because it undercuts their man-centered avenue to attaining righteousness. Catholicism is poised to confer grace through their numerous channels, but the doctrine of *sola fide* rips that away and allows individual sinners to go immediately to God and receive immediate divine imputation—all without the thralldom of Catholicism. Surely Luther was correct when he viewed Medieval Theology as bringing about the captivity of the church (*The Babylonian Captivity of the Church*, 1520). *Sola fide* springs the church free because individual sinners can be immediately justified by faith alone! As the modern automobile rendered the horse and buggy obsolete, so *sola fide* rendered useless the Catholic system of conferring grace to individual sinners. Unless Roman Catholicism can unequivocally affirm *sola fide*, we cannot unite with her because she denies the article of faith upon which the church stands or falls!

MARY

The Roman Catholic doctrine of Mary is another large obstacle to communion with Rome. When someone mentions Catholicism, the first thing that comes to most Protestant minds is their view of Mary. Don't they worship Mary? Good theologically schooled Catholics will vehemently deny that they do.[113] They argue that Mary is venerated (*dulia* or hyper-*dulia*) and not worshipped (*latria*).[114] But I suspect such a nuanced scholastic distinction is lost on most poor souls who pray to her.

---

[112] Bruce McCormack, "What's At Stake in Current Debates Over Justification? The Crisis of Protestantism in the West," in *Justification: What's at Stake in the Current Debates*, ed. Mark Husbands and Daniel J. Treier (Downers Grove: InterVarsity Press, 2004), 82.

[113] For example, see Karl Keating, *Catholicism and Fundamentalism: The Attack on "Romanism" by "Bible Christians"* (San Francisco: Ignatius Press, 1988), 268ff.

[114] Pope John Paul II bequeathed on his flock an Encyclical in 1983 entitled *Redemptoris Mater* (The mother of [our] Redeemer). Marian devotion is fully alive.

What do they believe? I will survey their doctrine concerning Mary and then critically appraise it. First of all, they believe Mary was immaculately conceived. But that has not always been believed. Men like Anselm argued that she was born *with* original sin; many after him actually argued that though she was *conceived* with original sin, she was nonetheless purified before birth (e.g., Bernard of Clairvaux and Thomas Aquinas). It wasn't until later that the Church declared her born sinless. In 1854, Pope Pius IX (in his papal Bull of Dec. 8, 1854— *Ineffabilis Deus*) declared that she was preserved from original sin. "We declare, pronounce, and define that the doctrine, which holds that the most Blessed Virgin Mary at the first instant of her conception, by a singular grace and privilege of Almighty God, in virtue of the merits of Christ Jesus, the Savior of the human race, was preserved immaculate from all stain of original sin...."[115]

Because Mary was "full of grace" (Lk. 1:28), they argue that she was "redeemed from the moment of her conception,"[116] (*CCC*, §491). Of course, they do not appeal to any explicit passage to argue this, but reason from this one verse to what must have been the case. However, most of the reasoning and support for this position are taken from tradition. They admit that though no explicit proof from Scripture exists, yet this doctrine was universally believed by the church, and therefore the doctrine must be true.

They also believe that she was assumed body and soul into heaven.[117] This does not mean she did not die.[118] Rather, after she died, her body and soul were taken into heaven. Vatican I did not declare this but the position was developed for years before it officially became the

---

[115] Denzinger, *The Sources of Catholic Dogma*, §1641 ("*ab omni originalis culpae labe praeservatam immunem*"). A papal Bull (*bulla*, a seal) was attached to an official pronouncement.
[116] Karl Keating actually tries to use the tense of the verse to substantiate immaculate conception. See his *Catholicism and Fundamentalism*, 268-270. He seems to conclude that the perfect passive participle of the word means "a perfection of grace." Any student of Greek will immediately recognize the folly of this.
[117] Ludwig Ott, *Fundamentals of Catholic Dogma*, 6th ed., trans. Patrick Lynch, (St. Louis: B. Herder Book Co., 1964), 208; Sylvester J. Hunter, *Outlines of Dogmatic Theology* (New York: Benzinger Brothers, 1894), 2:584. Hunter stated (note, this speculation existed before it became a matter of de fide), "Nevertheless, the belief in the bodily Assumption of our Lady after her death has long been generally accepted in the Church, and cannot be questioned without rashness" (2:586).
[118] Hunter, *Outlines of Dogmatic Theology*, 2:585 said, "There can be no question, therefore, but that the Blessed Virgin died...."

"dogma" of Rome in 1950 (Nov. 1, from a section in the 'Apostolic Constitution'). Pope Pius XII says in his *Manificentissimus Deus*:

> ...it seems almost impossible to think of her who conceived Christ, bore Him, nourished Him with her milk, held Him in her arms, and pressed Him to her breast, as separated from Him after this earthly life in her body, even though not in soul. Since our Redeemer is the Son of Mary, surely, as the most perfect observer of divine law, He could not refuse to honor, in addition to His Eternal Father, His most beloved Mother also. And, since He could adorn her with so great a gift as to keep her unharmed by the corruption of the tomb, it must be believed that He actually did this. . . . the august Mother of God, joined in a secret manner with Jesus Christ, from all eternity 'by one and the same decree' of predestination, immaculate in her conception, a most pure virgin in her divine maternity, noble ally of the divine Redeemer, who has gained full triumph over sin and its consequences, has finally attained as the highest crown of her privileges, that she should be immune from the corruption of the tomb, and that in the same manner as her Son she would overcome death and be taken away soul and body to the supernal glory of heaven, where as Queen she would shine forth at the right hand of the same Son of hers, the immortal King of Ages [1Tim. 1:17].[119]

The Biblical support is taken from Gen. 3:15. Namely, she participates in Christ's triumph over the effects of Satan. As Pius XII reasoned, it just seems preposterous to believe that Christ would let His own mother suffer the indignities of death. Some apologists argue that we do not have her bones and we would expect to have the bones of such an important person. Another explanation is that the Bible gives examples of Enoch and Elijah being taken into heaven without dying.[120]

To make matters worse, they call her a Mediatrix. Most Protestants would easily be offended by the suggestion that Mary was a Mediator. Yet, Catholic theologians have carefully crafted a doctrine that in some measure respects the teaching of Scripture (in the sense it reasons from some of the Scriptural principles) while at the same going far beyond it. "Like her Divine Son, though not in the same sense, Mary is an intermediary between God and His creatures....Hers is therefore a participated and secondary mediatorship...which derives its essence and

---

[119] Denzinger, *The Sources of Catholic Dogma*, §2331.

[120] Keating, *Catholicism and Fundamentalism*, 272-276.

effectiveness solely from the grace of Christ...."[121] In 1893, Leo XIII (in the Encyclical, "*Octobri mense*") said that "nothing at all of the very great treasure of every grace...is imparted to us except through Mary."[122] This was reaffirmed in the Second Vatican.[123] "Taken up to heaven, she did not lay aside this saving office but by manifold intercession continues to procure for us the gifts of eternal salvation."[124] Her mediation is entirely based upon Christ.[125]

The actual term probably became official with Leo XIII; it was definitely reaffirmed in the Second Vatican (*LG*, §62, "Therefore the blessed Virgin is invoked in the church under the titles of advocate, helper, benefactress, and mediatrix."). Some Catholic scholars wish to argue that the term "mediatrix" does not have dogmatic status, but that is hard to believe given the *Lumen Gentium* quote just cited. It at least has an implied support. They also cautiously state that she only served a "subordinate role" to Jesus.

How did they conclude that Mary is a mediatrix? Roman Catholic theologians argue that her consent to becoming the mother of God enabled her to become our spiritual mother (cf. Lk. 1:38). The Second Vatican talks about the "union of the mother with the Son in the work of salvation."[126] Not only in her consent ("her fiat"),[127] but also in her willingness to stand at the foot of our Lord (see John 19:25; cf. *LG*, §62) enabled her to become a mediatrix and some would argue, even our redemptrix. Quite revealing are these words: "She conceived, gave birth to, and nourished Christ, she presented him to the Father in the temple, shared his sufferings as he died on the cross. Thus, in a very special way she cooperated by her obedience, faith, hope and burning charity in the work of the Savior in restoring supernatural life to souls. For this reason she is a mother to us in the order of grace," (*LG*, §61). One theologian tersely summarized the Catholic position: "...because He sent His Word to us through Mary, it is right that we approach Jesus through Mary."[128]

---

[121]   J. Pohle, *Mariology: A Dogmatic Treatise on the Blessed Virgin Mary, Mother of God*, ed. A. Preuss (St. Louis: B. Herder Book Co., 1943), 22.

[122]   §1940a, id est, H. Denzinger, *The Sources of Catholic Dogma*, 488; in the Latin, H. Denzinger, *Enchiridion Symbolorum* (Barcelona: Editorial Herder, 1948), 541-542, "*nihil nobis, nisi per Mariam*."

[123]   *LG*, "Our Lady," §52-69.

[124]   *LG*, §62.

[125]   Pohle, *Mariology*, 121.

[126]   *LG*, §57.

[127]   This is the official phrase used in the CCC, §973.

[128]   Tanquerey, *A Manual*, 2:111.

If she is all this, how are they to respond to her? One Roman Catholic theologian argued that Mary is the mother of all men. She holds that honor because our Lord said, "Woman, behold thy son. Behold thy mother" in Jn. 19:26, 27. "When Christ constituted Mary the Mother of John, and John the son of Mary, he included the whole human race in the person of the beloved disciple. Thus, Mary has become our Mother, and we her children."[129]

As our Mother, they argue, she can receive our veneration (hyper *dulia*) while the other saints receive regular devotion (dulia) though God alone receives our worship (*latria*) [honor, respect, devotion vs. worship]. Devotion to her is "intrinsic to Christian worship" (CCC, §971). They can pray to her without offending Christ.

> A Catholic may confidently ask Mary for her powerful intercession without ever entertaining the foolish apprehension that there is danger of offending Christ by addressing Him through His Blessed Mother. The dogmatic teaching of the Church is too clear to allow any intelligent Catholic to believe that the Blessed Virgin is able to accomplish anything without her Son. In its last analysis, therefore, every prayer addressed to Our Lady is addressed to Christ, i. e., God.
> [130]

Mary forebears excesses and tolerates them (in her compassion), but the church will never let the "cult of the Virgin to obscure the dignity and majesty of Christ."[131] Pope Paul VI says, "We believe that the Holy Mother of God, the new Eve, Mother of the Church, continues in heaven to exercise her maternal role on behalf of the members of Christ," (CCC, §975). She is able to help the church because she is called the *abyss of grace*, the *sea of all graces*.[132]

Unfortunately, some Lutherans now believe that devotion to Mary and to the saints is permissible and not idolatrous.[133] That is a sad commentary on where some Lutherans are going, for once scriptural authority no longer controls ecclesiastical doctrines (as is the case with many Lutherans), then this defection to Mary is plausible and predictable.

---

[129]   N. O'Rafferty, *Instructions on Christian Doctrine: The Apostle's Creed* (New York: The Bruce Publishing Company, 1937), 166.
[130]   Pohle, *Mariology*, 131.
[131]   Ibid., 132.
[132]   Tanquerey, *A Manual*, 2:104.
[133]   Avery Dulles, *The Reshaping of Catholicism*, 234-235.

That Mary is Mediatrix is not enough for many devoted Catholics. Some call her *Redemptrix*. Roman Catholic scholars admit that these titles redemptrix and co-redemptrix were never used of Mary before the sixteenth century.[134] Yet, they do not shy away from implying, and for some explicitly declaring, that Mary is our co-redeemer. Pohle implies it: "The Blessed Virgin may be said after a fashion to have co-operated in the atonement, because she formed the Divine Victim in her chaste womb, prepared Him for the slaughter, and, standing beneath the Cross, offered Him up for the salvation of mankind."[135] Since the prophecy of Simeon indicated that a sword would pierce her soul, they reason that this supports their teaching that she suffered with her Son. Other Catholic theologians are more explicit. Tanquerey states that Mary is co-redemptrix because she co-operated (cooperatrix) in Christ's redemption.[136] He appeals to the same "proof-text" as Pohle.

The modern *Catholic Catechism* firmly focuses on her role "in the order of grace." They cite the official *Lumen Gentium* statement which argues that as ministers of the gospel share in Christ's priesthood, as creatures radiate the goodness of God, "so also the unique mediation of the Redeemer does not exclude but rather gives rise to a manifold cooperation which is but a sharing in this one source," (CCC, §970 citing *LG*, §62). In other words, as ministers share in the priesthood of Christ, so Mary shares in Christ's redemption; this is one of the manifestations of the "manifold cooperation" because of Christ's work and Mary's cooperation.

Officially, they have not adopted the title. They have, however, all but decreed that she is our co-redeemer. Mary is the counterpart to Eve; death came through Eve, life through Mary (*LG*, §56). It may not be long before she will officially receive the title.

There are other doctrines pertaining to Mary that could be seriously questioned. Her perpetual virginity and role as the mother of God are other examples.[137] A full-blown doctrine of Mary exists in Catholicism; the Marian dogma is coherent and is inextricably tied into all their other doctrines. Rather than critiquing each one individually, it is

---

[134]   Pohle, *Mariology*, 122.
[135]   Ibid., 122.
[136]   A. Tanquerey, *A Manual of Dogmatic Theology*, trans. Rev. Msgr. John J. Byrnes (New York: Desclee Company, 1959), 2:108-109.
[137]   Protestants debate *theotokos*. Most, however, affirm it but we cannot go into that in this paper.

better to raise principal theological objections that address all of them. So what are we to make of this Mariology? Though it can easily be argued that all these doctrines have absolutely no Scriptural foundation, there is still another way of critiquing them.[138] I will offer general theological critiques, and there are at least three major theological arguments that should be leveled against Marian dogmas.

The first one is the simplest. Their doctrine of Mary is inherently contradictory within their theological system. She is a co-redeemer and yet they maintain she was redeemed by Christ. She was immaculately conceived while in need of a Savior. Why would someone immaculately conceived need a Savior?[139] She is able to confer grace because she is full of grace and yet she is said to have been in need of grace herself. When they explain away one theological problem, they create yet another. Attempts to protect Christ's unique role by stating Mary's need of Christ are all undone when they elevate her soteriological roles in the church. Her Maternity trumps Christ's soteriology; Mary's motherhood looms larger than Christ's mediatorial work. These inherent contradictions are inevitable when they want both Scripture and Tradition.

The second critique is more important. Roman Catholic Mariology is the incarnation of synergism. It is the personification of their semi-pelagianism that has always vexed their soteriology. In Mary is found the Roman Catholic perfect example of human cooperation. So Karl Barth perceptively stated, "In the doctrine and worship of Mary there is disclosed the one heresy of the Roman Catholic Church which explains all the rest."[140] This one heresy explains, supports, and embodies all the rest of their other heresies. Mary is the paradigm of human cooperation, the one who helps in our salvation, the one who merited grace beyond measure, etc. She is the paragon of Man at his best, the embodiment of creaturely co-operation and free response to God

---

[138]   I am assuming that all Protestant readers can immediately see how the Roman Catholic Marian dogmas contradict Scripture and one can just as well read many good Protestant works that critique Roman Catholic doctrines from a Scriptural standpoint.

[139]   Cf. G. C. Berkouwer, *The Conflict with Rome,* trans. David H. Freeman (Philadelphia: Presbyterian & Reformed Pub. Co., 1958), 160.

[140]   Karl Barth, *Church Dogmatics,* trans. G. T. Thomson and Harold Knight, vol. I.2 (Edinburgh: T&T Clark, 1956), 143. He also stated that the "Marian dogma is neither more nor less than the critical, central dogma of the Roman Catholic Church, the dogma from the standpoint of which all their important positions are to be regarded and by which they stand or fall."

(remember her *fiat*). So Karl Rahner declared, "For she received salvation for us, by God's grace, but with true freedom, for us and for our eternal welfare." [141] These words rattle the godly sensibilities of all Protestants. Another Catholic writer wrote, "The dogma of the *Immaculata* means the proclaiming of what man was as a creature not yet fallen. It means the unpolluted face of the creature, the divine image in man...the creature's co-operation in redemption....On the humble *fiat* with which she (Mary) answers the angel hangs the whole mystery of redemption on the side of creation...." [142] She is considered to be the perfect Christian for us all because of her cooperation and example. [143]

Marian dogmas therefore best express everything our Reformers protested against in Roman Catholicism. [144] Luther's absolute intolerance to the Catholic doctrine of merit is embodied in Mary who is the example to all believers of how we are to cooperate with God. The Roman Catholic synergism in Erasmus and other Papists finds its ideal manifestation in the person of Mary. Striking down Marian dogmas demolishes the heart and soul of the Roman Catholic vision of salvation which is human cooperation.

The third general critique is that Mariology duplicates the person and work of Christ. [145] Mary plagues Christ and Marian dogmas function like leeches, sucking the very purpose and benefit of the person and work of our Lord Jesus Christ. Christ's work can never stand on its own. Mary duplicates almost every facet of Christ's person and work. The natural outcome of this leads to denigrating and devaluing Christ (though Roman Catholics vigorously maintain that they do all this *without* denigrating Christ and His work). Christ redeemed; Mary is our co-redemptrix. Christ is the Mediator; Mary is our mediatrix. Christ intercedes for us, so

---

[141] Karl Rahner, *Mary, Mother of the Lord,* trans. W. J. O'Hara (New York: Herder & Herder, 1963), 100.

[142] Cited in Karl Barth, *Church Dogmatics,* I.2, p. 145.

[143] Rahner says, "At last, a human being on this earth, an authentic, real human being, not an imaginary character in a novel, not the mere postulate of an ideal system of ethics, but a person of flesh and blood, with tears, toil, poverty, obscurity, but who is, wholly and utterly, purity, kindness, love, faithfulness, patience, compassion, and belongs to God alone, to such a degree that she 'merited'—as the Church goes so far as to say—to become the mother of the Redeemer, even though this 'merit' is a pure grace of God, the first grace that was imparted to her, and could not crown any previous merit," (*Mary, Mother of the Lord,* 80).

[144] Cf. Berkouwer, *The Conflict with Rome,* 164.

[145] I am greatly indebted to Berkouwer's penetrating analysis at this point; see his *The Second Vatican Council and the New Catholicism,* 221-248.

does Mary. We are taught to pray to Christ because He will supply us with His grace, so they tell us that we can also call upon Mary and she will enrich us from the vast treasure of her grace. Christ is the Second Adam; Mary is the Second Eve. Christ is at the right hand of God the Father; Mary is nestled right there as well. Christ is the King and Head of His Church; Mary is the Mother of the Church. Christ is the King of Heaven; Mary is the Queen of Heaven. Protestants call Christ the sure refuge of sinners, but Rahner called Mary the "refuge of sinners."[146] The examples could go on. All this robs Christ of the rightful glory and honor due to Him. If she does not usurp everything from Him then she certainly over shadows everything Christ does.

Barth is correct when he said that Mariology is the "one heresy...which explains all the rest." Vatican II did not overturn any of this and the new Catechism only reiterated their Marian dogmas. If Marian dogmas disappeared, then their doctrine of justification will disappear as well. Mariology is the article on which Roman Catholicism stands or falls.

THE POPE

Another critical doctrine is their doctrine of Papal infallibility. This was originally declared in Vatican I. When the Roman Pontiff should speak "ex cathedra" (from the seat) — "when carrying out the duty of the pastor and teacher of all Christians... [he] operates with that infallibility with which the divine Redeemer wished that His church be instructed in defining doctrine on faith and morals; and so such definitions of the Roman Pontiff from himself, but not from the consensus of the Church, are unalterable."[147]

We are very familiar with this doctrine. This itself bars us from coming into communion with the Roman Catholics because we believe only God and His utterances (His Word) are infallible. Good books have been written to refute this.[148] There is just one thing we need to consider on this topic. All the ecumenical attempts must concede this one point, namely, that the Pope is their leader. Richard John Neuhaus, one of the

---

[146] Karl Rahner, *Mary, Mother of the Lord*, 82.
[147] Denzinger, *The Sources of Catholic Dogma*, §1839, p. 457 (*Enchiridion* [34th edition], §3073).
[148] The classic is George Salmon, *The Infallibility of the Church*, 4th ed. (1914). Also, consult the helpful volume by Norman Geisler and Ralph E. MacKenzie, *Roman Catholics and Evangelicals: Agreements and Differences* (Grand Rapids: Baker Book House, 1995), 203-220.

principle leaders of ECT, was asked by *Modern Reformation* the following question, "Can you conceive of a scenario in which there would be visible unity of the various Christian bodies without the pope as its head?" Neuhaus answered, "If you ask, can one conceive of full communion among Christians that does not include the exercise of Petrine ministry clearly grounded in the New Testament, instituted by our Lord to be a center of strength and guidance for the brethren, then the answer to that is no, because that would be contrary to our Lord's intention."[149]

The ecumenical dialogue between Anglicans and Catholics (ARCIC II)[150] produced a document called "Church as Communion." In it, they suggest that full unity can only occur when there is some acknowledgement of the Roman Primate.[151] Similar language is found in their dialogue with Lutherans.[152] If and when they would merge (in the last phase), the following would hold true: "The merged church would have only a single bishop." There simply can be no final visible unity unless the Pope's rule is acknowledged.

Here is why this is significant. All doctrinal concessions on the part of the Roman Catholic Church, whatever they are, even *sola fide*, are moot points if the Pope is the head. It is like setting up an irrevocable trust. All your property and wealth are in the trust and the appointed trustee is your son. He promises fealty, care, and will have in mind your personal interest. But once the trust has been set up, he controls everything and in the end, your entire welfare is in his hands. It may work out well and it may not. It would be spiritual suicide to come under the absolute authority of a mere man.

OTHER DOCTRINES AND WHY WE CANNOT UNITE

We could list other important doctrines that still divide us. Their views of sacraments, indulgences, purgatory, saint worship (veneration), their ecclesiology, use of the rosary, etc., are all problematic. But some say, "There is so much we have in common." It is true! But we have also

---

[149]   Anon., "An Interview with Father Richard John Neuhaus," *Modern Reformation* 14:5 (September/October 2005): 34.
[150]   The Second Anglican-Roman Catholic International Commission.
[151]   "In the context of the communion of all the churches the Episcopal ministry of a universal primate finds its role as the visible focus of unity…Local churches recognized the necessity of maintaining communion with the principal sees, particularly with the see of Rome." See Gros, Meyer and Rusch, ed., *Growth in Agreement, II*, 340.
[152]   See Gros, Meyer and Rusch, ed., *Growth in Agreement, II*, 472-475.

noted that this has always been the case. Noll and Nystrom listed several examples of commonality. But strong view of scripture, salvation by grace, christology, Trinity, etc., have never been the subject of debates. The Reformers recognized all those things in Catholicism. For them and for us, what was principally at stake was the gospel! Justification by grace alone through faith alone because of Christ alone...not all the *solas* are affirmed by the Catholics, especially *sola fide*.

Does that mean Catholicism will not change? Not at all. I think she will change, but not for the better. The poison of liberalism is already in her blood stream. Unless they do some theological blood transfusion, they will eventually become like all the main line churches. Joseph Ratzinger (the current Pope Benedict XVI) seems to be arresting the liberal tendency in his sect. Surprisingly, he has finally allowed the use of the Latin Mass, which is nothing more than a shrewd political move to reign in and retain all the hard core traditionalists. If Ratzinger gets his way, then we'll have a clearer and more traditional Roman Catholicism with which to deal. If he fails to control the trend, then the liberalizing universalistic form of Catholicism will go to seed and we certainly could not fellowship with that. It seems to me, the only way we can "unite" with them is for Catholicism to change and become Protestant in her doctrine. This may sound narrow and uncharitable, but this is a battle over the very heart of the gospel.

WHAT DOES THIS MEAN AND WHAT SHOULD WE DO?

In the mean time, we still need to consider some practical steps. How are we to approach Catholics? Can we fellowship with them? How should we view them? Are they our brothers and sisters? I will give a handful of suggestions.

1. *Rome is not part of the visible church, but does have real believers.* Given their view of justification, Mary, semi-Pelagianism, and the Pope, along with the liberalizing universalism in their theology, one is hard pressed to see how they could be part of the visible church. Do any of the three marks of the church exist in her? She may fall under the large umbrella of Christendom, but they are not part of the visible church (if we can make such a distinction).

True believers may dwell in her midst, and I'm convinced that many ignorantly remain in her. But that does not make Roman Catholicism a part of the visible church. Once those believers recognize the difference, God's Spirit will lead them out. No doubt many will protest and give anecdotal accounts of "true believers" they have met over the years in Roman Catholicism. I would neither disagree with them nor deny those things, but that does not make the institution Christian or part of the visible church anymore than saying, "Well, I am friends with several genuine believers who work for Microsoft, Inc." Who would deny that? That does not in any way may Microsoft a Christian organization. The original question must be answered. Is the genuine gospel preached? No. Does she rightly administer the sacraments? No. Does she faithfully discipline? No. We are led irrefutably to the conclusion that Roman Catholicism is not part of the visible church.

2. *We should lovingly evangelize Catholics.* Contrary to what ECT I stated (namely, that we should not proselytize "it is neither theologically legitimate nor a prudent use of resources for one Christian community to proselytize among active adherents of another Christian community."), we need to reach out to them with the gospel. Are there not efforts on their part to "convert" Protestants? Indeed. We must assume that not all Catholics are believers. We may run into one or two who are, but they are the exceptions and not the rule. Many of them may be moral, religious, and very devout, but those things are not true indicators. Perhaps it is not proselytizing that needs to be done as much as evangelization.

3. *Social co-belligerence—yes, but as individuals and not as "churches."* Because the Roman Catholic faithful are moral and hold to many traditional moral standards, we should have no problem working with them as public citizens of the State. We can be co-belligerent while we as individual citizens of the State seek to affect some good. However, this does not mean that specific local churches ought to work with Catholics. It is one thing for individual Christians to labor with a faithful individual Catholics, but quite another thing to lock arms with them as two spiritual institutions.

4. *Know your doctrine.* Because of their media efforts and recent converts, many Catholics are becoming quite conversant in defending and propagating papist doctrines. Some of them know their Bibles very well and can argue cogently. Though their arguments are no different from some of the older Roman Catholic apologists, many of them are well aware of the glaring weaknesses in evangelicalism. Evangelical ignorance of doctrines makes them sound very persuasive.

It is important that each true evangelical believer know what he or she believes. It may require probing some theological truths more deeply to see how they differ from Catholicism. Some of us learn our truths much better in contrast to systems of error. Not only should we study more and become well grounded, we should most of all endeavor to deepen our vital union with Christ. Genuine spiritual communion with our Lord as we meditate on solid theological truths will do more for our souls than any of the allures of Catholicism. When we are weak here, we become spiritually vulnerable.

5. *We may need to re-baptize.* Given our first point, we may think long and hard on this important question. Do we need to re-baptize Catholics? Without resurrecting the Hodge-Thornwell debate,[153] we can ponder this with greater clarity. The one advantage we have over our well studied godly forefathers is Vatican II. I'm convinced Hodge would have a different opinion about this debate if he were alive today. Vatican II, as we have argued, fundamentally altered Catholicism. She is not the same as the one Hodge and Thornwell knew. Catholicism is more problematic than before and as a result I cannot see the validity of Catholic baptism. Unlike fine wine, she has not improved with age.

6. *Study the "Ten Theses for Roman Catholic-Evangelical Dialogue."* Finally, I recommend the ten points found in *Modern Reformation* entitled, "Ten Theses for Roman Catholic-Evangelical Dialogue." I appreciate these affirmations and denials and conclude with a summary of those propositions: 1. Although both Evangelicals and Catholics affirm the ecumenical creeds, it does not follow that Catholicism is a true visible expression of Christ's body. 2. The evangelical doctrine of justification still prevents us from having any genuine fellowship with those who oppose the gospel (i.e., Catholicism). 3. Though Evangelicals can cooperate with Catholics in certain areas, this does not mean we have a common mission, a common church, and the same gospel. 4. The needs of the age should not determine the mission of the Evangelical church or serve as the basis for ecclesial communion with Catholicism. 5. Christ's prayer for unity is not limited to the spiritual and visible church. 6. Unity

---

[153] See James Henley Thornwell, *The Collected Writings of James Henley Thornwell* (1881; reprint, Vestavia Hills, AL: Solid Ground Christian Books, 2006), vol. 3; the same content is published as James Henley Thornwell, *Sacramental Sorcery* (Unicoi, TN: The Trinity Foundation, 2006), but we recommend buying all of Thornwell.

must be determined by the Word of God and unity cannot be achieved in the absence of a common gospel. 7. Though some Roman Catholics may be our brothers and sisters in Christ, we still cannot have ecclesial union with Catholicism. 8. No gospel convert should remain in a church where the Word is not rightly preached and the sacraments are not rightly administered. 9. Though Catholicism may contain true believers, we still deny that Catholicism is itself a true visible congregation. 10. We believe that what still divides us is very important and our common cultural engagement cannot override those foundational differences.[154]

---

[154] "Ten Theses for Roman Catholic-Evangelical Dialogue," in *Modern Reformation* 14, no. 5 (September/October 2005).

Chapter 6

The Christian View of War

Richard D. Phillips[1]

"He does not bear the sword in vain. For he is the servant of God, an avenger who carries out God's wrath on the wrongdoer." Romans 13:4

On March 9, 2003, former President Jimmy Carter published an editorial in the *New York Times* condemning the American invasion of Iraq. Carter argued that this was not a just war. Clear alternatives to war did exist, he said, and the United States lacked the proper authority for its stated aim of imposing a regime change in Iraq. Moreover, he charged that the violence inflicted would be out of all proportion to any harm our nation has suffered from Iraq and that a great number of civilian casualties would be likely. Carter thus stated that it was "an almost universal conviction of religious leaders" that the American invasion did not constitute a just war, writing off conservative evangelical dissenters as being wrongly "influenced by their commitment to Israel based on eschatological... theology."

---

[1] Richard Phillips M.Div. is Senior Pastor, Second Presbyterian Church (PCA) in Greenville, SC and on the Executive Staff of the Alliance of Confessing Evangelicals.

I have not conducted a scientific poll, but among the great number of evangelical Christians I know, a very high percentage came to the opposite conclusion than the one offered by former President Carter. They, and I, would argue that war was the only credible option left, and that Iraq's support of terrorism and weapons of mass destruction posed a grave threat to American security. We would point out that American forces went to every extreme to minimize enemy casualties and damage to property, and especially to safeguard the lives of civilians. Obviously, Carter did not ask me or the religious leaders I know, because our "almost universal conviction" was exactly opposite to his.

My point in referencing Carter's editorial is not to debate the American involvement in Iraq. More broadly, his comments show that when it comes to Christian views of war and other matters of national policy, one's assessment may have more to do with whether he or she is a Democrat or a Republican and whether he watches CNN or FOX News, than with whether he or she claims to be a Christian. But Christians must reflect biblically, not just politically, on the subject of war. Most believers will never give a political speech or write an op-ed piece for the New York Times, pontificating on the justice of this or that political event. But as Christians we will talk with people around us. We will shape the experience of wartime for our children. And we will come before God in the secret place of prayer. Those who preach and pastor churches will lead prayer meetings and give biblical instruction on such matters as the current war. All of these call on Christians to reflect on war in the light of God's Word.

THE NECESSITY OF WAR

The place to begin is by asking, Are wars necessary? And by implication, Is it necessary for Christians to serve in the armed forces? The majority of people today, including some Christians, would probably answer that wars are not only evil and destructive but also unnecessary. The pacifists, especially, cry out, "We don't have to fight wars!"

But the perspective revealed in the Bible takes the other position, namely, that wars are necessary in this present evil world. Not that war is *desirable* – for it is not – but that war is *necessary*. J. Douma summarizes: "Surely the Bible is not pacifist. Numerous wars were fought at God's command or with His approval (see Num. 21:14 and Dt. 20:16-18, also Rev. 19:11), so that we can hardly characterize war with the generalization that it is *sin*."[2] This does not make war an activity that we should consider normal; we should never look upon times of war as "the good old days," although for a number of reasons we often do. Douma states, "War is an abnormal business... Although Scripture presents no prohibition against waging war, the Bible does make clear that war and bloodshed must never be accepted as normal phenomena (see Mic. 4:1-5). King David was not allowed to build a temple for God because he had waged war and had shed blood."[3]

But despite all the suffering and hardship it inflicts, war is necessary because of the existence of evil in this world and because of the Christian duty to stand in opposition to evil, especially in its most organized forms. The fact is that we live in a world that Paul characterized as "following the prince of the power of the air, the spirit that is now at work in the sons of disobedience" (Eph. 2:2). Christians ought not look at footage of the Nazi rallies prior to World War II and ask, "How does this happen?" If we read our Bibles, we know how this happens. It happens the same way Adam and Eve happened to eat the forbidden fruit in the garden: it happens because there are evil spiritual powers at work in this world. Now that man is fallen into the totally depraved state of sin, war happens because, as Paul also said of fallen mankind, "Their feet are swift to shed blood; in their paths are ruin and misery, and the way of peace they have not known" (Rom. 3:15-17).

I know what it is like to stand before the television watching blood-thirsty mobs crying out for mass murder and ask, "How can people be like this?" But the very fact that I am astonished reveals that my mind has not yet been sufficiently transformed by God's Word. In the world described by the Bible, nations will need to defend themselves from violence from their neighbors, and especially righteous nations will need to arm themselves to oppose wicked nations.

PACIFIST OBJECTIONS

Experience shows, however, that Christians do not all agree with this point of view. All biblically-minded Christians are agreed on the sanctity of life and the prohibition against murder. But what are we to think of military service and capital punishment? During the history of the church, orthodox theology has supported both of these as consistent

[2]   J. Douma, *The Ten Commandments* (Phillipsburg, NJ: P&R, 1996), 239.
[3]   Ibid., 239-240.

with a Christian's duty. But a strong tradition of Christian pacifism has also developed and seems to be attracting many adherents today. It particularly seems that many young Christians – concerned about war and disenchanted with what they perceive as a politically-motivated evangelical establishment – are attracted to Christian pacifism.

One of the main tenets of Christian pacifism is to argue that the coming of Jesus Christ has abrogated the Mosaic Law. But this is a false premise. Jesus makes clear that his teaching did not set aside God's moral law but rather gave its true exposition. "Do not think that I have come to abolish the Law or the Prophets," he declared; "I have not come to abolish them but to fulfill them" (Mt. 5:17). Moreover, citing the Sermon on the Mount, pacifists argue that Jesus set aside the "eye-for-an-eye" mentality of the Old Testament.[4] Just as Jesus explained with regard to divorce, saying that it was an accommodation to the realities of sinful life (Mt. 19:8), pacifists argue that the death penalty and the Old Testament's endorsement of war do not reflect God's true intention. While God does not change, they say, his way of relating to mankind does change. So while killing could be considered lawful in the time of Moses, in the age of Christ it has been replaced with an absolute law of non-violence.

However, if God's provisions for capital punishment and warfare in the Mosaic Covenant truly did not reflect his own will, but were merely an accommodation to human weakness, how do we explain that God himself commanded capital punishment and war in the Old Testament? Unlike his mere toleration of divorce – which God certainly never demanded – God mandated both capital punishment and warfare all through the Mosaic economy. Moreover, the imagery of war is prominent in the Book of Revelation's celebration of Christ's final victory: "Then I saw heaven opened, and behold, a white horse! The one sitting on it is called Faithful and True, and in righteousness he judges and makes war... He is clothed in a robe dipped in blood" (Rev. 19:11-13).

In reading Christian pacifists, one encounters deeply impassioned writing and forceful arguments from Scripture. When it comes to the sixth commandment, most Christian pacifists argue that it

---

[4]   In pacifist writings, however, the "eye-for-an-eye" principle is generally misunderstood. In the Mosaic Covenant, the purpose of requiring an "eye-for-an-eye" was not to encourage vengeance but to restrict it.

must be understood through the lens of Jesus' teaching in the Sermon on the Mount as well as through the example of Jesus' life. The pacifist will say, "I agree with your description of the world but not with the remedy. Jesus has told us to respond to the power of evil by demonstrating the power of love." Jesus' teaching of non-retribution – turning the other cheek – is thus enshrined as a universal ethic for every category of human engagement. Instead of fighting, pacifists argue, we ought to allow the wicked to oppress us as an opportunity for us to witness the gospel.

The question, then, is whether or not non-retaliation is, in fact, the remedy that the Bible proposes for nations and societies in response to the threat of evil. The answer is that it is not. When Jesus was sending his disciples to labor for his sake in the world, he told them, "Let the one who has no sword sell his cloak and buy one" (Lk. 22:36). And, in Romans 13:4, Paul clearly informs us that the civil government must bear the sword on God's behalf to establish justice and punish evil. Paul says that the civil ruler bear the "sword" on God's behalf. He "is the servant of God, an avenger who carries out God's wrath on the wrongdoer" (Rom. 13:4). That same passages tells Christians that they have a duty to obey the civil ruler in his discharge of this divine mandate.

An analogy between the state and the family is illuminating. To admit that war is necessary to the state is the same as to admit that a father is duty-bound to defend his children. Were the pacifist ideal consistently applied it would call for a father to stand by while his little son or daughter was physically assaulted – a monstrous proposition. It is no less monstrous to propose that a civil leader entrusted with the care of the general population should stand by and allow them to suffer violence. It would seem, therefore, that we must properly relate Jesus' teaching of individual non-retaliation with the Bible's teaching on the duty of the state to bear the sword. In attempting this, C. S. Lewis called for individual Christians to embrace Jesus' mandate for non-retaliation. But he added:

> Insofar as the only relevant facts in the case are an injury to me by my neighbour and a desire on my part to retaliate, then I hold that Christianity commands the absolute mortification of that desire. No quarter whatever is given to the voice within us which says, 'He's done it to me, so I'll do it to him.' But the moment you introduce other factors, of course, the problem is altered. Does anyone suppose that Our Lord's hearers understood Him to mean that if a homicidal maniac, attempting to murder a third party, tried to knock me out of the way, I

must stand aside and let him get his victim? I at any rate think it impossible they could have so understood Him.[5]

To deny the necessity of war in a world like ours is to deny our duty to be our neighbor's keeper and to fail to love our neighbors as we ought to love ourselves. It denigrates the impulse of protection of life enshrined in the sixth commandment and sunders the covenantal bonds of mutual responsibility on which society depends.

THE SIXTH COMMANDMENT

The Sixth Commandment confronts the taking of human life. In the Hebrew of Exodus 20:13 it consists of two words: "No killing." This is variously translated in our Bibles as "Thou shalt not kill" (KJV) or "You shall not murder" (NKJV, NIV, ESV).

The Bible introduces death as the consequence of disobedience to God. The first time the word "die" appears in the Bible it is found in God's warning: "You may surely eat of every tree of the garden, but of the tree of the knowledge of good and evil you shall not eat, for in the day that you eat of it you shall surely die" (Gen. 2:16-17). This prompts the reflection that the entire subject of an end to human life involves an abnormality, and an abnormality arising from sin. The subject of death is introduced in the form of a warning and its appearance arises from the retributive justice of God. Mankind has a death problem because we have a sin problem.

It is not surprising, then, that murder is one of the immediate results of the fall; indeed, murder appears as the quintessential result of man's alienation from God. When Adam and Eve's first son Cain was refused by God for bringing the wrong offering, his anger manifested itself in taking his brother Abel's life. And as the root of sin grew deeper in man's spirit, murder was not only practiced but celebrated. The first song ever recorded by man was a gangster rap ditty from the mouth of Lamech: "I have killed a man for wounding me" (Gen. 4:23).

God expressed his disapproval of murder in clear terms. Cain was cursed for killing Abel: "The voice of your brother's blood is crying to me from the ground. And now you are cursed" (Gen. 4:10-11). Further condemnation of Cain and Lamech's culture of death appeared in the great flood that washed clean the earth.

---

[5]   C. S. Lewis, "Why I Am Not a Pacifist," in *The Weight of Glory and Other Addresses* (New York: MacMillan, 1975), 50.

With this background, it is not surprising that the sin of murder features strongly in God's covenant with Noah after the flood: "Whoever sheds the blood of man, by man shall his blood be shed, for God made man in his own image" (Gen. 9:6). This enshrines the principle of the sanctity of human life and also provides its rationale. The life of man is to be preserved upon pain of death. It is so great a sin to murder a human that the act must be punished by the loss of the murderer's life. The reason for this is not utilitarian but theological: "For God made man in his own image." Every single human being was made to declare God's praises and possesses this high potential and calling. That which was made in the image of God must be held sacred. This idea of the sanctity of human life is essential to our appreciation of the sixth commandment. But our application of this principle must recognize that in enshrining this principle, God himself has enshrined as well the just taking of human life, grievous though this may be. Biblically, the just taking of human life is established precisely because of the sanctity of human life.

It is this principle of the sanctity of human life that finds expression in the sixth of God's Ten Commandments. It is noteworthy, I think, that when we consider the two tables of the law, containing our duties to God and our duties to man, the sixth commandment is the first and founding obligation to our fellow humans.[6]

First, we must always exegete the text. The question is, "Does the sixth commandment prohibit all killing, or does it prohibit murder, that is, the unjust taking of human life?" Should Exodus 20:13 read, "Thou shalt not kill," as the King James Version renders it, or "You shall not murder," as most translators phrase it today? Does the Sixth Commandment prohibit all killing prohibited or just a certain kind of killing?

A brief study of the original text will yield an answer. The Hebrew language has at least eight words for killing and the one used here is significant. Philip Ryken explains, "The word *ratzach* is never used in the legal system or in the military. There are other Hebrew words for the execution of a death sentence or for the kind of killing a soldier does in mortal combat. Nor is the word *ratzach* ever used for

---

[6]   Many today hold that the second table of the law – our duty to man – begins with the fifth commandment, enshrining the authority of parents. But this does not seem to have been the understanding in biblical times. In my judgment, the fifth commandment should be taken as the last of our duties to God, involving as it does our obedience to God through divinely established authorities.

hunting and killing animals... What the commandment forbids is not killing, but the unlawful killing of a human being."[7]

John Murray adduces reasons to understand the sixth commandment as not forbidding all killing but only unlawful killing. Mainly, he notes the context in which the Ten Commandments were given, that is, the Mosaic Covenant. Murray argues,

> The Mosaic revelation, which had the Decalogue at its center, prescribed the death penalty for a great many offences, and the sixth commandment could never have been understood as prohibiting the infliction of death as retribution for certain sins. Any argument against capital punishment based upon the sixth commandment does not have even the semblance of plausibility; it could be used only by those who abstract the sixth commandment from the total context in which it appears."[8]

By rightly defining the meaning of the sixth commandment, we can see that it 1) is based on the sanctity of human life, since man bears the image of God; 2) prohibits the wrongful taking of human life; and 3) implicitly establishes conditions for the rightful taking of human life. These reflections must provide the basis for all of our subsequent discussion of capital punishment and war.

THE PURPOSE OF WAR

Turning to consider the purpose of war, we find this embedded in the reality of war's necessity. If war is necessary to oppose and overthrow evil in this world, especially when that evil marches under force of arms, then the purpose of war must be to promote life and peace in opposition to evil. If it be observed that this situation proposes a cruel irony – that war is the way of peace – the irony is no less than that found in God's command to Noah, "Whoever sheds the blood of man, by man shall his blood be shed" (Gen. 9:6).

First, we should be clear on wrongful or unjust purposes for war. God has not given the civil authority the sword in order to extend its own nation's power, or to act out one nation's hatred against another, or to ensure a sufficient and economical supply of oil. War is not necessary as a way of shaping public opinion prior to elections nor as a program for perpetuating manly virility in succeeding generations. This last proposal

---

[7]   Philip G. Ryken, *Written in Stone* (Wheaton, Ill.: Crossway, 2003), 136.
[8]   John Murray, *Principles of Conduct* (Grand Rapids: Eerdmans, 1957), 113.

is one that has often been advanced as a purpose for war. Francis Bacon, for instance, wrote that war provides exercise to a nation's character in the same way that physical exertion does to the body. He wrote, "No body can be healthy without exercise, neither natural body nor politic: and certainly to a kingdom or estate a just and honourable war is the true exercise."[9] The fact that this rationale was later espoused by Adolf Hitler is no recommendation. Instead, the true purpose of war is expressed by J. Douma: "The goal of war must always be peace, and any program of armament must be pursued in the context of preserving peace."[10]

This reminds us that God is glorified in war only when war serves his cause of life and peace. Psalm 29:11 connects the blessing of armed might with its intended blessing of peace: "May the LORD give strength to his people! May the LORD bless his people with peace!" God commands, "Turn away from evil and do good; seek peace and pursue it" (Ps. 34:14). St. Augustine therefore wrote, "War is waged in order to win peace. Hence, even in warfare, be a peacemaker that you may by conquering your assailants, bring them over to the advantages of peace... Let it be necessity, not your desire, which slays the foe in fight."[11] If the warrant for war lies in the sixth commandment's mandate of the sanctity of life, then the ends of war must be consistent with a commitment to the sanctify of life, along with its dignity and blessing. Moreover, the manner in which a nation wages war must be calculated, so far as possible, to minimize the loss of life and to cultivate a post-war peace.

I have the privilege of descending from a military family. My father served in the Army for 30 years, fighting in the Vietnam War, and my grandfather served on active duty for forty years, serving in both World Wars and in other conflicts. I am the short-timer, having served under arms for only 13 years. God has blessed me with two sons, and I hope that they, too, will serve God by taking their places in the ranks of our nation's men-at-arms.

I was talking about this to my oldest son, and I made the comment to him that it is the glory of American war-making that the enemies we vanquish in war have typically become our closest allies and friends after the war. In the heartland of America there are German

---

[9]   Cited from William Barclay, *The Ten Commandments* (1973; Louisville: Westminster John Knox, 1998), 72.
[10]   Douma, *The Ten Commandments,* 240.
[11]   Augustine, *Letters to Boniface*, Letter 189.

enclaves that began with prisoners-of-war in the Second World War who did not want to return home after their internment in America. America has waged war with the aim not of domination but of mutual peace and prosperity. And the way America historically wages war is designed to promote those very ends. Surely this is one of the reasons why God has blessed our arms so singularly during the 230 years of our existence as a nation.

It is for this reason that I have been so horrified at the recent rhetoric surrounding the idea of the torture of captives in our present war against terrorism. I realize that isolated incidents of torture have always taken place in war. I also admit that I do not know the details of what has taken place in our present war and that media accounts may be deceptive. What I do know is that many public figures, some of them high government officials, have suggested that the dangers of our situation warrant the use of torture. This violates the nobility that has been embedded in our military tradition and can only reflect the advanced barbarity that has grown in our society. Moreover, a nation that tortures its captives has forgotten the aim of peace. Torture creates multi-generational enemies; it fosters hatred and violates the image of God with which even the most hardened terrorist has been born. If America is to continue to wage war in a manner that is biblically defensible, we must repent of even the suggestion that we may or ought to practice torture as part of our way of war.

Securing a more stable peace is the main purpose of just war, but there is another purpose that should not be neglected, namely, just retribution. People don't like to think this way today. To execute a guilty murderer or to wage a war of punishment is thought to be contrary to pursuing the ends of peace. But the Bible specifically notes just retribution as a purpose for which the state is given the sword. Paul says that rulers are to be a terror to bad conduct and are to be feared by those who do evil. "He is the servant of God, an avenger who carries out God's wrath on the wrongdoer" (Rom. 13:3-4). Peter teaches that rulers are sent by God "to punish those who do evil" (1 Pet. 2:14). John Calvin drew a direct analogy between the criminal punishment of offenders within the state and the military punishment of offending nations: "Whether it be a king who does it on a big scale, or a scoundrel who does it on a small scale, he is equally to be regarded and punished as a robber... The slaying of the authors of an unjust war is an execution, the judge is God, and the fighting men who defend the right are merely God's instruments."[12]   Throughout the books of Joshua, Judges, and Samuel, this is precisely the Bible's perspective on the use of armed might to strike down wicked oppressors.

THE JUSTICE OF WAR

The scope of this chapter will not permit an extended treatment of just war theory, although much has been imbedded in what we have already considered. It follows that if a war is to have godly purposes, then it must be waged in a righteous manner. So what are the standards by which Christians assess the justness of a war?

St. Augustine is generally credited with outlining the main contours of just war theory that have prevailed in Christian thought. First he addressed the issue of motive: war must be waged for the right reasons, namely, an ultimate desire for peace both by protecting against evil-doers and by punishing them. Augustine wrote, "It is wrong to doubt that war is righteous when it is undertaken in obedience to God, to overawe or crush or master human arrogance."[13]   This means that, in general, wars of conquest are not just, despite the various rationales provided.

Moreover, war must be conducted under rightful authority. It is not just anyone who can launch a war, but only the rightful civil magistrates appointed under God's providence. This is often a serious issue in wars of revolution and rebellion, which require a demonstration that a new and just authority has been established in the place of one made illegitimate by negligence or abuse. Such was the authority under which American colonists ended British misrule.

War ought to be waged with a reasonable opportunity for success, and the violence involved must be proportional to the injury suffered. These are categories in which there will often be disagreement. For instance, many will cite the use of atom bombs at Hiroshima and Nagasaki as singular abuses in the latter category. Yet those bombs were dropped was to quickly end a war that threatened a long and even bloodier climax. Furthermore, just war theory demands that every effort be made to avoid civilian casualties. This does not mean that civilian lives are worth more than those in uniform. But it does argue that in a

---

[12]   John Calvin cited in Barclay, *The Ten Commandments*, 69.
[13]   St. Augustine, *Against Faustus*.

just war, violent force will be applied as closely as possible to those who threaten violent force, so that civilian casualties are avoided as much as possible. We see the difficulties of this, however, on television almost every night. Just invaders wrestle against enemies who deliberately employ civilians as shields and against a media that delights to present pictures of every civilian casualty as an indictment of the policies of war.

The application of the rules of just war are not always cut-and-dried, and there will always be some debate about how well a particular situation fits with just-war theory. An example is the debate over our nation's present war in Iraq. But Christians will find these to be helpful guidelines for considering future conflicts. What are our motives? Are there feasible alternatives? Is the cause worth the risk and the damage? We should never assume that might equals right; indeed, Christians should be among the first not only to support a just government but also to exhort it in the cause of justice, especially in war.

THE GLORY IN WAR

Having considered the necessity, purpose, and justice of war, a Christian appraisal ought also to consider the idea of glory in war. Those are two words regularly associated: war and glory. On Veterans Day, small towns across America hold parades featuring medal-bedecked veterans who bask in the glory of their armed exploits. Is this right? Does this promote wrongful violence?

Let me argue that while war itself is not glorious, it is indeed the arena in which much of the glory of the image of God in mankind is displayed and rightly celebrated. The Christian general Robert E. Lee is reported to have remarked on the bloody field of Fredericksburg, "It is good that war is so terrible; otherwise we should love it too much." That was a candid and understandable statement, rightly observing the irony of virtue and love so often displayed amidst scenes of carnage.

There is glory in war – it is the glory of the virtue that leads soldiers to sacrifice themselves to things that are just and true. The glory found in war is celebrated by the great war song of Jesus' mother, Mary, also known as the *Magnificat*. Perceiving victory in the great battle through the birth of her Savior Son, Mary sang:

> My soul magnifies the Lord, and my spirit rejoices in God my Savior. For he has looked on the humble estate of his servant. For behold, from now on all generations will call me blessed; for he who is mighty has done great things for me, and holy is his name. And his mercy is for those who fear him from generation to generation. He has shown

strength with his arm; he has scattered the proud in the thoughts of their hearts; he has brought down the mighty from their thrones and exalted those of humble estate; he has filled the hungry with good things, and the rich he has sent empty away. He has helped his servant Israel, in remembrance of his mercy, as he spoke to our fathers, to Abraham and to his offspring forever (Lk. 1:46-55).

Here, Almighty God is celebrated for his triumph in cosmic holy war. But notice that God is glorified not merely in his might, but mainly in what his might has done. He has regarded the humble and poor. He has achieved great things for those in need. He has stood up to the proud hearts who would exalt their strength over the weak, throwing down their thrones and establishing justice in their place. He has confronted the evil order and turned it back. He has acted with strength in mercy, and in faithfulness to his covenantal bonds.

These are the elements of the only real glory in war. True glory in war consists not in what is destroyed but in what is preserved, not in battles that are won but in the righteousness upheld by those battles, not in the riches that are taken but in the wealth that is bestowed, and not in the number of casualties inflicted but in the life that is defended. The glory we should seek in war is that of devotion to duty in a righteous cause so that a godly legacy may be preserved for those who will follow. These are the things that God cares about, and the reality is that war, for all its horrors, is a fitting arena in which praise may be offered in faithful service to God, so that he is glorified by our good and valorous deeds.

THE END OF WAR

In sum, war finds its true purpose not in death but in the lives and in the life that are defended and held sacred. Just war is necessary because of sin and because of the sanctity of life enshrined by the Sixth Commandment. Therefore, even in war – indeed, especially in war – Christians must always be aiming for life. What a challenge this is when the instruments of war are mainly agents of death – bullets, bombs, mines and bayonettes! The Civil War general James B. McPherson cried out, "If to be a soldier is to lose my humanity, I do not want to be a soldier." Therefore, to be a Christian soldier, one must cultivate his God-honoring humanity – his care for life, his refusal to exult in death, his restraint in the use of force, and his faith in God that can stand up to the rigors of passion and fear.

War is necessary, so let those called to war devote themselves to study battle and train for war. War can be just, so let those who fight for just causes take satisfaction in their cause. War can be an arena in which much true glory – as well as false – can be gained and displayed. But according to the Bible, the end of wars will one day come. Do we rejoice in this prospect? Even as we devote ourselves to war-making, do our hearts yearn for the garden and the plow, when the excitements of battle are no more? Let warriors above all guard the wellspring of their hearts, training them by faith for the end of war when Jesus returns, and let their battles be fought and won in service to the end of war he will someday bring.

The prophet Joel spoke words fitting for our present evil age: "Proclaim this among the nations: Consecrate for war; stir up the mighty men. Let all the men of war draw near; let them come up. Beat your plowshares into swords, and your pruning hooks into spears; let the weak say, 'I am a warrior.'" (Jo. 3:9-10). That is a call to arms. But its point was to summon for judgment all those who trust in the sword and whose delight is in the sharpness of the blade. The Christian soldier must cultivate a different heart, by the plow of God's Word and the power of God's Spirit. The Christian who fights for life in this world looks forward to life in the world to come in which all fighting and strife will have ceased.

The prophet Isaiah gave us a glimpse of a great day to come when war shall have ceased because sin shall have been expelled from a world renewed by the light of God. He wrote, "They shall beat their swords into plowshares, and their spears into pruning hooks; nation shall not lift up sword against nation, neither shall they learn war anymore" (Isa. 2:4). With this end in mind, while we train for war let us learn to practice peace, for this is the end for which all just war serves. And as we practice war – for we must in this present evil age – let us look to our reward not in what the sword can win us, but in the day when the sword shall be re-forged as a plowshare, and when out of the warring nations a new humanity in Christ will be joined in bonds of brotherhood for a peace that will never end.

Chapter 7

Print and Pixels: How They Mediate Our View of the World

Gregory Edward Reynolds[1]

Have you ever asked yourself how your cell phone or your television affects your worldview? Few people do, but Christians should. In *Leadership Journal*, editor Marshall Shelley exhibits a media naiveté that inhibits the development of a consistent Christian worldview. Here is what Shelley says:

> For the past year we've been exploring the overarching theme of "The Church and Culture," and one thing that has become clear: the church is entering a new era. As Andy Crouch of our Christian Vision Project puts it: "We're entering the third age of the human race. The first was 'orality,' where people communicated primarily by oral, spoken language. The second was literacy, when suddenly, after Gutenberg, the printed page became the main means by which culture was shaped and imaginations were formed. Now we're entering a third age: the age of visualcy." ...our world is accustomed not just to "visualcy" but to connectedness." [2]

Along with explaining new features of the new format of *Leadership* and its addition of "print plus" *Leadership Journal* online, Shelley looks

---

[1] Greg Reynolds D. Min. is Pastor of Amoskeag Presbyterian Church (OPC) in Manchester, New Hampshire.
[2] Marshall Shelley, "What're You Lookin' At?" in *Leadership* (Winter 2007), 7.

ahead explaining that these changes have caused him to discover a third step in sermon preparation:

> What do we want people to *see* while we're preaching. What visuals will we add to our formerly spoken-word-only experience? Photography? Video? Classic art? A symbol?
>
> An upcoming issue of *Leadership* is going to deal with the technology of preaching and how to preach the Word in an image-driven culture.[3]

Correcting this media naiveté, however, is fraught with difficulty for several reasons. First, Americans are generally addicted to novelty, and thus naively captivated by every new invention, assuming that if there is a problem it is with the user and not the invention. Second, the church is so invested in electronic culture that to alter the connection would be so painful and require such self-denial that few would be willing to make the break.

The Shelley quote illustrates precisely why I titled my book: *The Word Is Worth a Thousand Pictures: Preaching in the Electronic Age.* Shelley makes several wrong assumptions: 1) that preaching and the latest visual technology are compatible; 2) that without some visual technology there is nothing to *see* in the preaching moment; 3) that Andy Crouch's analysis of the history of communication technology is accurate; and 4) that we are more "connected" today than ever before. Furthermore, there is a serious omission: any discussion of major theological questions we need to ask about worship and the church in their relationship to the electronic media. But Shelley's naiveté is not a problem affecting only worship and preaching—that is serious enough in its own right—but also powerfully yet subtly affecting every dimension of Christian life. Thus, the way we view the world—our worldview—cannot be complete with standing back and understanding media.

The lack of meaningful discussion among Christians, especially Christian leaders, on this subject is due to the almost complete absence of understanding of the nature of technology as extensions of man, or, in particular, electronic technologies of communications. This is where it is critical to understand Marshall McLuhan's famous aphorism "The Medium is the Message."

---

[3] Ibid.

THE MCLUHAN DICTUM: "THE MEDIUM IS THE MESSAGE"

The concept of a medium's being inextricably related to the message it communicates is inherent in the reality of both the Creation and the Incarnation. The form of things cannot be separated from their substance. To understand media properly, form and content must be analyzed together. One problem is that like fish in water we are too close to the electronic environment to observe and be aware of it. Since media affect the way we see the world—having become the lens through which we view things—they tend to go largely undetected, a kind of stealth element in our worldview reminiscent of the fifties movie *The Invasion of the Body Snatchers* (1956), in which unseen, undetected aliens invade human bodies. We are, as McLuhan says, somnambulists sleepwalking through life, being transformed by media—by our inventions—without being aware of it. Developing awareness is therefore essential.

For example, we are regularly told that public speaking is an inferior form of communication. Ninety nine out of a hundred Christians, educated or uneducated, thoughtful or not so thoughtful, say Oh, yes, preaching is a foolish way to communicate—that's what Paul says in 1 Corinthians 1, right? No, that is what our culture says, but not what Paul says.

The KJV, unintentionally and also unfortunately for modern readers, gives that impression in its translation of 1 Corinthians 1:21: "it pleased God by *the foolishness of preaching* to save them that believe" (emphasis mine). For Paul, along with all of the ancient world, there was no more powerful and respected means of communication than public rhetoric. The ancients developed it into a fine art, and many of the great preachers of the ancient church, like Augustine and Ambrose, were trained as debaters and rhetoricians. So effective was this medium that Paul's statement is in the midst of a warning not to confuse the power of the gospel with "lofty speech" (1 Cor. 2:1). The ESV clarifies the meaning nicely: "it pleased God through the folly of *what we preach* (NKJV foolishness of *the message preached*) to save those who believe" (emphasis mine). The cross, not public speaking, is the folly rejected by unbelief (v.18).

A man speaking, especially a pastor, is the only appropriate— and I would say God-ordained—medium for the message of the good news of God Incarnate, since "the Word became flesh and dwelt among us..." (John 1:14). Preaching by a pastor is the primary medium chosen by God to communicate His Word and thus form the mind and life of his people. I am using the concept of medium in the broadest sense here. The use of electronic media in preaching, such as PowerPoint, modifies the message in ways unintended but no less pernicious.[4] It brings the message of business and mass consumption into the church. What may be helpful for a missionary presentation outside of worship is not helpful in worship. Edward Tufte has a thorough critique of the weaknesses of PowerPoint in the business world.[5]

So the medium—every medium—is an essential aspect of every message. Our inventions are not good or evil—but neither are they neutral. McLuhan spoke of media as extensions of man. So the telephone is an extension of the ear and the voice. Each medium has its suitability or message, along with both intended and unintended consequences. I regularly hear Christians assert that television is evil, or the Internet is just a tool that we can use in different ways. However, we should think of media in terms of what they are created to do, and then learn to assess their liabilities and their benefits. If all inventions are extensions of man, then rather than assume that they are just tools that we use either for good or ill, we must ask how our inventions may be shaping us. That is to say that if we assume that we are in control of our inventions we will never ask what the messages of our inventions are, and thus they will change us in subtle ways of which we are largely unaware, because not only does the medium affect the message, but it also changes us—our worldview—and the organization of the world itself.

Another way of thinking about this issue is that each medium is more than a mere conduit of information. This is usually where Christians end their analyses, e.g., there is too much sex and violence on TV, implying that their elimination would make TV good. But that analysis deals with the medium only at its most basic level: as a conduit of information—the medium itself being irrelevant to the message, as if the message would be the same no matter what the medium. Joshua

---

[4]   See my book, *The Word Is Worth a Thousand Pictures: Preaching in the Electronic Age* (Eugene, OR: Wipf and Stock, 2001), chapters 8-10 for elaboration of this point.

[5]   Edward R. Tufte, *The Cognitive Style of PowerPoint* (Cheshire, CT: Graphics Press LLC, 2003). The NY Times called Tufte the "Leonardo da Vinci of data." A statistician who has thought deeply about the visual presentation of data. A pointed critique of a technology that exemplifies the problem of technique overwhelming substance. Tufte actually demonstrates how technique is often a substitute for good content, and good teaching, person to persons.

Meyrowitz's media metaphors can help us go beyond this. He points out that all media of communication may be viewed through the lens of three different metaphors: conduit, language, and environment.[6]

So then "The Medium Is the Message" means that each medium changes the way we receive or "view" the message, becoming an integral part of the message. The different elements—the language or grammar—used in producing communication through a given medium change the message. Take, for example, the grammar of television. What are the unique production variables in television? The camera is an element you don't see, but you see through. In a television debate, like the presidential debate between Richard Nixon and John Kennedy, the way those faces were communicated through that scene—the expressions and camera angles—is the grammar of that medium. What is not shown by the program manager is also very significant. Apparently, while those who saw the debate on television thought Nixon lost, those who listened to it on the radio thought Nixon won. The grammar of radio focuses the mind, through the ear, on the content of what is said. The language of television focuses on faces and people and is thus a poor medium for religion or objective truth of any sort. This brings us to the next metaphor.

Finally, "The Medium Is the Message" means that each medium changes the way we view the world, ourselves, and the way we live in the world. This environmental concept is complex and multi-faceted, and thus more difficult to grasp and easier to ignore. Social space is reorganized by the media of communication. Media create, and are part of, a total environment. As an environment it draws us into itself, but is also connected with the whole fabric of cultural reality of which we are a part. Media are extensions of man which make up an essential element of the social fabric and culture of human life. McLuhan wanted to get us to see how media change our perception of the world around us.

The proverbial "fifteen minutes of fame" reflects the way media change our self- perception and our sense of social space. Where such a

---

[6]   Joshua Meyrowitz, "Images of Media: Hidden Ferment—and Harmony—in the Field," *Journal of Communication* 43, no. 3 (Summer 1993): 55-66. See *No Sense of Place: The Electronic Media on Social Behavior*. New York: Oxford University Press, 1985. Meyrowitz has gone beyond McLuhan, through his study of situational sociologist Erving Goffman (*The Presentation of Self in Everyday Life* 1959), to show that the media of communication and transportation change social structures. Postman's *The Disappearance of Childhood* builds on Meyrowitz's insight that the television in particular has changed the social institutions and interrelationships of our culture.

concept originate? No one would have ever entertained that concept before television or radio. Mass media make the difference. The assumption is that if millions of people see you on a television screen, something very important is happening, when in fact it may be—and usually is—quite trivial. This changes the way that you look at reality for good or ill. For example, religion on television gets muted and altered by the focus on people and the commercial and entertainment environment of the medium. There is much to consider here.

The old boundaries distinguishing childhood from adulthood have disappeared.[7] An extreme example of the alteration of social space is the problem of sexual predators and child pornography on the Internet. Perverse human nature is exacerbated by the new medium. Such intrusions into family life were not possible before the Internet, but parents are caught unaware because of the prevalent media naiveté.

A more subtle example of changing self-perception is revealed in a recent Associated Press article titled "Study: U.S. youths stuck on themselves," with the subtitle " 'I'm special': Psychologists say the narcissism factor is rising."[8] The electronic media tend to foster an extreme self-absorption and desire for self-authentication. Rather than finding lasting meaning and significance in actual community, they seek the fleeting rewards of the virtual.

Stepping back and becoming aware of media is essential to good stewardship of those media. A simple place to begin is an analysis that I call the BLT—the Benefits & Liabilities Test. For example, what are the benefits and liabilities of electronic mail? It is helpful for quick document transfer, messages for meetings, and such. Part of the message of the e-mail medium is efficiency. Messages to people we already know well face-to-face may be especially helpful. But among its liabilities are its tendencies to lessen or eliminate face-to-face communication, to encourage sloppy thinking and composition, and to open new possibilities for misunderstanding. Email lacks the complexity required in important personal communication. It is also too easy to send trivial and even annoying messages that clutter our lives and diminish real human contact. Its message is "I'm fast and easy." An e-mailed note of condolence or even an apology, however well meant, would convey, "I don't care enough about you to take the time to write, call, or visit."

---

[7]   See Neil Postman, *The Disappearance of Childhood* (London: Allen, 1983).

[8]   David Crary, "Study: U.S. youths stuck on themselves," *New Hampshire Union Leader*, February 27, 2007.

In summary, "the Medium is the Message" means that all media particularly all communication technologies, change the way that we perceive and relate to the world—that is to say, media radically affect our worldview by affecting the message we are receiving or seeking to communicate. Since media are the subtle windows through which we view and relate to the world, we as Christians are called to be stewards of media, what McLuhan called media ecologists.[9] This has become an essential application of the Christian calling to be transformed, because iff we ignore the nature of media we will be conformed to this world in ways of which we are unaware. Romans 12:1-2 is an inspired appeal to pay attention to the influences of the world in which we live: "I appeal to you therefore, brothers, by the mercies of God, to present your bodies as a living sacrifice, holy and acceptable to God, which is your spiritual worship. Do not be conformed to this world, but be transformed by the renewal of your mind, that by testing you may discern what is the will of God, what is good and acceptable and perfect."

To be unaware of the media environment and influence is to be conformed to it. Romans 12:1-2 commands us to be transformed, the only antidote to world-conformity. The ways in which we each implement media stewardship will vary, so I want to be clear that my own applications of this principle are not commands of Scripture, but what I think are wise implementations of this command. But the command itself must be heeded.

PROS AND CONS: A CONSIDERATION OF TWO MEDIA

In seeking to gain media awareness it is helpful to think about a pre-electronic medium. The place of printing in history is an excellent place to begin, recognizing that print is a relative new-comer on the media scene. Chirography, or handwriting, has been around since about 3500 BC. It began as a simple pictograph or logograph, which pictured objects and ideas. The development of syllabary writing, using consonants, can be seen as early as 1500 BC in the Hebrew and Phoenecian languages. Then in the early first millennium BC phonetic writing, including the invention of vowels, was developed by the Greeks. Printing in which moveable type was first employed began in the Western world with the inventor Gutenberg in 1450 AD. Electronic

---

[9] Neil Postman and many others have expanded this legacy and formed the Media Ecology Association formed in 1998. See *The Word Is Worth a Thousand Pictures*, 119.

communication began in 1844 with the telegraph. Samuel Morse's exclamation upon receiving the first message was "What hath God wrought!" The wise Christian—a media ecologist—turns this into a question: What has God wrought? Common culture is a mixture of God's cursings and blessings. He expects Christians to distinguish between the two.

PRINT PROS AND CONS: A CONSIDERATION OF PRINT AS A MEDIUM

Print exhibits at least seven important characteristics, which I have observed, and which will help focus on how to analyze a particular medium. First, print is visual. The letters on a page must be seen. They are images which in themselves are works of art. Men like Anton Janson, Frederic Goudy, Stanley Morrison, and Bruce Rogers made typography into a fine art. Letters and words are abstract symbols of speech. The difference between digital words and printed words is that the former are mediated by electronics and often mixed with visual images that are non-intellectual.

Second, print is rational and logical. It fosters organization and tends toward bureaucratic control. It also tends to undermine memory, as Plato predicted, because it commits words and ideas to paper for storage, rather than requiring retention in the memory. The oral question and answer format of catechism, memorization of Scripture, and other forms of recitation can help overcome this liability.

Third, print is historical. A book or pamphlet has a beginning and an end, a characteristic it shares with writing. Print has thus facilitated the writing of history. The idea of linear history is uniquely biblical, and print has tended to foster this Augustinian understanding of history.

Fourth, print is concrete and permanent, affirming the reality of space and time, as a kind of incarnation of speech, even as speech is an incarnation of thought. It is a physical object to be possessed on a page, and in a book. It is not easily changed as with electronic words in word processing, thus tending to make the writer more thoughtful and careful.

Fifth, print is private. It can be used to undermine tradition, an example being its use in the Reformation to undermine the authority of the Roman Catholic Church. It spread knowledge to everyman, thus democratizing learning and authority. Some Protestants, unaware of this tendency, have given way to the "pope in every heart," setting up the individual as the final arbiter of truth. But, positively, print deepens individual understanding, because the reader is able to reflect on a text at his own pace. Meditation and reflection are necessary for spiritual formation. This is fostered in deep or efferent reading, that is, reading from which one takes derives something useful and soul-expanding. Thus it tends to contribute to the public or communal good. (cf. #7 below).

Sixth, print is slow-paced and thus reflective. The pace of print is conducive to deep reading—to contemplation and thoughtfulness. In comparing high and low resolution television one discovers that black and white is low resolution, thus inviting the viewer to imagine and fill in the blanks. High resolution leaves very little to the imagination. The printed word is a visual medium with extremely low resolution, allowing and even inviting one to stop and reflect, and even connect with the inner world of the reader. The lower the resolution, the more the viewer/reader supply with his imagination.

Finally, print is public or communal. It may be passed on to another generation in exact form. Texts of communal importance bind communities together. The formation of a substantive inner world enhances connection with the outer world and community. This was especially so when most believers received the word by hearing only, instead of reading. In the centuries before the invention of the printing press, neither Christians nor Jews, with rare exceptions, owned Bibles privately because of the expense of reproducing texts (all copied by hand, so Scripture was literally the "writings"). The Bereans did their Scripture searching in the synagogue (Acts 17:10–1 1). Originally these writings were not read silently and privately as we usually do with print, but were predominantly read aloud in public.

PIXELS PROS AND CONS: A CONSIDERATION OF ELECTRONIC MEDIA

First, an image and pixel culture is not of the devil, but neither are they an unmixed blessing. Remember that pictures are printed in books and texts are formed by pixels. God's Spirit enables us to "see through" the printed image to the transcendent reality. Print, while an image, tends to "see through" into the invisible mental world, as well as maintaining us in the concreteness of space-time reality. While pixels can be a means of drawing us into another virtual world that may lead toward idolatry, they have also enhanced typography and thus print as a medium.

Second, there are many pixel environments, divided into public and private realms. The personal computer and its word processor is one very common private environment. But the Internet connects pixels to a public, mass environment. These environments may be either more passive, like television, or more interactive, like the Internet.

Third, the world of pixels provides us with complex networks of images and information. Thus obscure texts once available only through extensive travel are now widely available. Obscure journals have worldwide audiences. Small churches receive messages from far away places. But this very efficiency also scatters attention. Email is too easy to send, often overwhelming the recipient. (See 6 below.)

Fourth, as a means of mass communications, the Internet can be a dangerous tool of propaganda and control, not only for governments, but also for consumer capitalism and radical individualism, including financial and sexual predators. Jacques Ellul understood the danger for the Christian and the church's evangelistic calling when he said: "People manipulated by propaganda become increasingly impervious to spiritual realities."

Fifth, pixels—those little points that make up images and text on computer and television screens—tend to mesmerize—"pixelate"—us into believing that this present view of reality that we see is all there is. What we see tends to limit us to this world—by capturing our attention and bewitching us into a virtual world. They lead us in, enchanting, carrying us along, mesmerizing and enthralling, often drawing us into thoughtless experience. By contrast, good literature asks one to consider or examine its content at some level. It draws you in order to change you and expand your soul. In contrast, some pixel-using media such as video games tend to privatize experience in ways that do not enhance the communal, but radically diminish it.

Sixth, the pace of pixels—connected with the entire electronic network—is fast and even simultaneous. Multi-tasking has become a new concept based upon this "all-at-onceness." McLuhan coined this term to point out the characteristic of simultaneity in the nature of electricity. This effect is not limited to electronic technologies: the front page of the newspaper exhibits this. Since the advent of the telegraph, disparate, context-less information has been scattered over the page. Each item has little or nothing to do with the others. The rapid the pace tends to undermine thoughtfulness and deep, reflective reading. There is always email, the weather, or the stock market to check. This has dramatically increased the pace and complexity of modern life generally, tending to spread our consciousness more thinly. One wonders how much this pace has contributed to maladies such as ADD and "road rage."

Seventh, pixels tend to encourage a laissez faire, "whatever" attitude. People are influenced more by pictures than by words. Word processing makes words ephemeral, lacking authority and permanence, and thus disposable, undermining respect for forms. Words have become too easy to delete. Email is worse. "It's just words," or "It's just talk" are common platitudes of our culture. Words are evacuated of meaning. Images then "inform" us with unassailable impressions, often at the emotional level, rather than cultivating clarity of thought as print tends to do. Pixels on TV and the Internet are used to mute truth and homogenize information in order to appeal to a mass audience. Conciliation is the mood pixels foster. Building market share is often the goal. Thus, commercial interests tend to dominate.

Eighth, pixels tend to democratize and undermine authority much more radically than print. Why should one heed anyone else? Everyone has his say, no matter how inferior his ideas. On the other hand, pixels also have been used to undermine totalitarian government and rationale. We have seen the demise of the media dominance by the traditional major networks. It will be interesting to see how Islam fares using the electronic environment of the west, for the relativizing tendency of pixels may dilute its authoritarian claims. China is discovering that consumer capitalism and the electronic media together are an indomitable force undermining totalitarianism. The legitimate authority of the church and the family are also threatened by this duo.

Ninth, pixels tend toward Gnosticism, a denial of the essential goodness of the created order. The production of virtual realities diminishes understanding of the concreteness of God's creation. McLuhan referred to this tendency as "disincarnation." The "virtual campus," for example, is literally a utopia—no place.[10]

So Christians ought to develop the ability to reflect in similar ways on all of the inventions of man in order to be better stewards of culture. The imposition of modernity by the electronic media is relentless, and only those who hone the skills of media stewardship will maintain biblical perspective in obedience to the command of Romans 12.

---

[10]   See *The Word Is Worth a Thousand Pictures*, 305-308.

BE A GOOD STEWARD OF PRINT AND PIXELS—OF WORDS IN EVERY FORM

McLuhan's main didactic thrust was to make people aware of the effects of media on people and culture. Christians who wish to view the world through the lens of God's Word, must develop something akin to McLuhan's ecology of media that will at once inoculate them against cultural conformity and cultivate an attractive counter-environment. What follows is an outline of that pursuit.

It is essential to keep in mind several biblical facts about language—to develop a theology of language. All human language has its origin in heaven, points to heaven, and is a revelation of God. The first words were spoken by God: they were powerful utterances effecting creation *ex nihilo*. Then God spoke to Adam, whom he had created in His own image, establishing the Adamic covenant through oral communication. Man's speech is thus patterned after God's. From this beginning of speech we discover two unalterable realities which are especially important to affirm in the postmodern climate which views human nature as completely malleable: 1) the human nature uniquely made in God's image, and 2) the world God has made. All of fallen man's distortions and corruptions cannot obliterate these two irrevocable realities, however much damage he may inflict on himself and others in attempting to do so.

Remember also that written words are a technology capturing speech—oral words—in space and time. Printed words are a technology capturing oral and written words for an extensive "audience". Finally, electronic words are a technology manipulating oral and printed words in a variety of new ways.

In light of his biblical view of language, the Christian is called to be a good steward of words in every form, pixels and print included. We are called to assess and prize words in all forms as God's gift. Poetry, for example, is not generally popular in the milieu of rationalistic science, but comes into its own in oral culture. That is why there is so much of it in the Bible. We should pay attention to the patterning of words as the incarnation of thought, and we should become wordsmiths, craftsmen of this great gift of communication. This is in turn a stewardship of all of our relationships, most of which are created, cultivaed and sustained by verbal communication, whether oral, written, printed, or in pixels. How are we to do this?

ASSESSING THE PROBLEM BY ASKING
THE RIGHT QUESTIONS

We should begin by asking the right questions and acting accordingly. How does this or that medium or electronic environment enhance or diminish my relationship with God, others, and creation?

Let us begin at the horizontal level by asking: How does a particular medium or electronic environment enhance or diminish my relationship with others? The more personal a medium is, the more affective the communication will be. I use the term "medium" loosely here—as I did referring to the preacher's humanity as a medium above— as anything through which a message is communicated. I do this because, made in God's image as we are, and Jesus being the <u>Media</u>tor between God and man, the medium of communication is our humanity. More narrowly speaking, media of communication are technologies of man, mechanical and electronic. The personal aspect of the medium is a function of the message of the medium itself, as well as the context in which the message is presented or sent. For example, if I already know someone face-to-face, an email message will be more personal, and perhaps more comprehensible to the recipient. It will be better communication because the foundation of a personal relationship has been established. The truth is, the larger the audience, the less personal the communication. This is true even if it is sent to you personally, but not written or meant for you only. This is the character of mass media of all kinds and why I usually delete all emails sent to a distribution list. As the late journalist Marya Mannes (1904-1990) said it, "The more people are reached by mass communication, the less they communicate with each other."[11]

Despite all the talk of "connectedness," electronic communication tends to undermine community generally. For example, consider this recent headline: "Online forums replace coffee shops for farmers."[12] The article shows a smiling farmer in his office glued to a computer screen. After lauding the benefits of online forums the journalist adds: "Some farmers still rely on the neighbor they know." If everyone "communicated only online" there would truly be no

---

[11] Marya Mannes, "Thought for Today," *New Hampshire Union Leader*, January 4, 2007, http://www1.bbiq.jp/quotations/communication.htm.

[12] "Today's Almanac: Thought for the Day," *New Hampshire Sunday News*, February 11, 2007.

neighbors. Communication implies community, which in turn implies space-time communing with other human beings.

Electronic communication also tends to undermine the community of the church. Professor Quentin Schultze notes that his students at Calvin College seem increasingly incapable of speaking of serious matters face-to-face. How will such students relate to the community of the visible church? How much face-to-face Christian fellowship and general human contact is undermined by our electronic way of life? As my wife and I walk in our old neighborhood, we meet fewer and fewer people and see more and more the blue haze of television and computer screens emanating from houses with large front porches, on which we rarely see people. Within those houses almost everyone is "connected" with a screen, but not the very people with whom they "live." The church must deliberately be different, and the present environment offers us a remarkable opportunity to demonstrate something of the beauty of true community.

A second and most fundamental question we need to ask is: How does a specific medium or electronic environment enhance or diminish my relationship with God? How does God command us to worship him and hear his word? In worship it is important that we use all of our God-given senses: seeing, hearing, touching, smelling, and tasting; what we see should be the God-appointed servant—a living man—representing his Savior as a vicar of God's people, as a pastor who cares for them; hearing the pure Word of God; seeing, tasting, and touching the Lord's Supper. I believe the Reformed Regulative Principle of worship prohibits electronic intrusions such as PowerPoint.[13] Such electronic media tend to eclipse and alter the message of the gospel and the message of the majesty of God communicated by worship itself.

The Internet breaks down formality and undermines God's structure of authority. For example, I received a letter of transfer from a fellow minister that began: "Dear Greg," and it was signed with a first name. I had to go to my church directory and make sure I knew who the person transferring was and what church he was leaving. . I responded with a diplomatic note, reminding the pastor that we needed an official letter of transfer and asking that he attach such a document to an email, trying to make it easy. To this day I have not heard, or seen, a word— that was years ago. The point is that a simple formality—a very

---

[13] See *The Word Is Worth a Thousand Pictures*, 300-305. See my comments on PowerPoint above under the first heading.

important structure in our Presbyterian way of doing things—is being undermined by the ease of email. That is only a little illuminating detail of what is happening throughout our culture and in our churches—innocent in one way, and yet truly pernicious.

The Electronic environment is also undermining deep reading, which directly affects the church and its worship, especially preaching. Dana Gioia, chairman of the National Endowment for the Arts, in introducing the 2004 report "Reading At Risk: A Survey of Literary Reading in America," warned:

> While oral culture has a rich immediacy that is not to be dismissed, and electronic media offer the considerable advantages of diversity and access, print culture affords irreplaceable forms of focused attention and contemplation that make complex communications and insights possible. To lose such intellectual capability—and the many sorts of human continuity it allows—would constitute a vast cultural impoverishment.
>
> ...Reading develops a capacity for focused attention and imaginative growth that enriches both private and public life. The decline of reading in every segment of the adult population reflects a general collapse in advanced literacy. To lose this human capacity—and all the diverse benefits it fosters—impoverishes both cultural and civic life.[14]

ACTING ON OUR ASSESSMENTS BY DEVELOPING A COUNTER-ENVIRONMENT

McLuhan's solution to the problem of the electronic environment was to create what he called a "counter environment." His was an individualistic concept. What I am suggesting here is a more corporate, ecclesiastical idea. In the context of the mediating institutions of the church and the world, a counter environment exists and must be maintained as an antidote to being swallowed up by the whole—an inoculation against the overwhelming power and influence of the so-called "connected" world. Developing a personal immunity to the liabilities of the electronic environment is imperative for the Christian's true community in relationship with God and others. The following is an outline of some of the elements necessary for the counter environment.

---

[14]   "Reading At Risk: A Survey of Literary Reading in America," Research Division Report #46 (Washington, DC: National Endowment for the Arts, 2004) http://www.nea.gov/pub/ReadingAtRisk.pdf.

Cultivate deep reading, writing, and conversational skills. Deep reading develops the inner life. The act of reading deepens and extends the self because the printed word, at its best, provides a continuing conversation with the great ideas of the past and the present, ideas which connect us with our culture and beyond. Such reading expands the soul in its connectedness with creation, culture and cultus.

Sven Birkerts emphasizes the importance of "inwardness," or to use Ong's term, "interiority." The older definition of sensibility is related to such inwardness, meaning "of a refinement or cultivation of presence; it refers to the part of the inner life that is not given but fashioned: a defining, if cloudy, complex of attitudes, predilections and honed responses....Here is the power, the seductiveness of the act: When we read, we create and then occupy a hitherto nonexistent interior locale."[15] Cultivating inner resources is the business of God's image bearers. Sinners do so solely for their own purposes, and find there a giant God-sized void, which can never be filled even with the craftiest human fashioning.

For the Christian this enterprise of soul-expanding study is essential to spiritual formation and thus a delight. The Psalmist both experienced and longed for this inwardness in the profoundest way: "You desire truth in the inward parts, and in the hidden *part* You will make me to know wisdom" (Ps. 51:6). Such inner development builds a treasure from which the Christian may contribute significantly to the church and to the world.

Literacy is essential to Christians not for reading the Bible alone. That is where we begin, because we must interpret all else through its teachings—but it must not be where we end. As Calvin observed, we see the world through the spectacles of Scripture. A good education affords us access to the great conversation of the ages of recorded history, the intelligent world in which the Lord has situated us, and called us to be his witnesses to the light. Then we come full circle to a richer understanding of God's Word as relevant in all ages and cultures.

Another way to cultivate the counter environment, but which space does not allow me to elaborate, is the practice of the arts of letter writing and conversation. These constitute a dying art and stand out as supremely personal in contrast to word processing and email. No one writes like you. Carefully chosen stationery and good penmanship

---

[15]   Sven Birkerts, *The Guttenberg Elegies: The Fate of Reading in an Electronic Age* (Winchester, MA: Faber and Faber, Inc., 1994) 87.

communicate genuine care and humanity. Conversation is advanced by good reading and writing. Nothing fosters community like face-to-face communion.[16]

More specifically, we must cultivate the counter environment of the church. Reform the Mass if you will—not the Roman Mass as we did 500 years ago—but mass culture and media. Electronic media used in the context of genuine community tend to mute its liabilities and enhance its benefits. This suggests that print and preaching be given particular priority as media for developing a Christian worldview.

Protecting and developing reformed and biblical worship and preaching is the most potent ingredient in the inoculation process. Good readers make thoughtful listeners who bring much to the business of hearing sermons, and thus take much of significance away with them, and into the life of the family, the church, and the community. "Reading," Stephen Webb observes, "is actually a form of hearing."[17] I am ultimately pleading for a kind of efferent listening, which can only be cultivated through the same kind of worthwhile reading. Oral and written communications go hand in hand, and we need aform of preaching that requires the effort of both preachers and hearers of the Word.[18]

The Reformation conception of preaching is stated lucidly in the *Second Helvetic Confession*: "The preaching of the word of God *is* the word of God." Our Lord, the incarnate Word, has identified the preaching of His ordained spokesmen with His Word: "He who hears you hears Me" (Luke 10:16). Romans 10:14 should be translated as the *American Standard Version* has it: "And how shall they believe in Him *whom* they have not heard?" as opposed to "Him *of whom* they have not heard?"[19] Thus it is "the preached Word rather than the written Word" which is the primary means of grace.[20] Properly understood Christ is immediately present as the true Speaker in the preaching moment. "The implication is that Christ speaks in the gospel proclamation."[21] Calvin comments on the

---

[16]   See *The Word Is Worth a Thousand Pictures*, 271-277.
[17]   Stephen H. Webb, *The Divine Voice: Christian Proclamation and the Theology of Sound* (Grand Rapids: Brazos Press, 2004), 29.
[18]   See *The Word Is Worth a Thousand Pictures*, 313-400. Note especially "The Excellencies of Preaching as a Medium," 333-345.
[19]   David H. Schuringa, "The Preaching of the Word As a Means of Grace: The Views of Herman Hoeksema and R. B. Kuiper." (Th. M. thesis, Calvin Theological Seminary, 1985), 18-22. Later in chapter III (34-43) a convincing case for the grammatical correctness of this translation is made.
[20]   Ibid., 33.
[21]   Ibid., 43.

same passage: "This is a remarkable passage with regard to the efficacy of preaching...."[22] Preaching is not speaking about Christ, but is Christ speaking to his people. It is the powerful voice of God—the Good Shepherd of the sheep. "The voice of the LORD is powerful; the voice of the LORD is full of majesty" (Psalm 29:4).

Lose yet another generation of good readers and you lose another generation of good listeners.[23] What can we do? Sounding the alarm is only the beginning of a solution. We should initially encourage a disciplined use of passive and interactive electronic media. What must follow is a concerted effort by church leaders and parents to cultivate discerning reading of a wide range of the best literature. We should also encourage reading aloud and discussion of what is read. We must encourage discussion of sermons. We must help the young find the joys of deep reading and attentive listening.[24] We must also teach them to understand media.

We must, therefore, also help train a generation of preachers who know how to communicate the text of Scripture in a winsome, interesting, and spiritually convicting way. So preachers must carefully distinguish between literary and oral presentations.[25] Soon, then, there will be hope that the next generation of the church will fall in love with God's Word.

Preachers should cultivate skills in public rhetoric. May it not be said of us that "people today are not tired of preaching, but tired of our preaching."[26] Ministers should be ministers of the Word and words—wordsmiths. If words spoken and printed are the incarnation of thought, then the greatest care must be taken in crafting them into sermons—the speaking of the Word. Ideas are only as good as the words that articulate them and give them form. Our commitment to Confessions and Catechisms is a commitment to a form of words, as memory work assumes. As Paul reminds Timothy: "Follow the pattern of the sound

---

[22]   Ibid., 44; John Calvin, *Epistle to the Romans*, Vol. 19 of *Calvin's Commentaries*, 22 vols. (repr., Grand Rapids: Baker Book House, 1979) 398.

[23]   Gregory Reynolds, " 'Reading At Risk' means Preaching At Risk," *Ordained Servant* (February 2006) http://opc.org/os.html?article_id=6.

[24]   See "Hearts of Flesh: The Committed Hearer," *The Word Is Worth a Thousand Pictures*, 345-352.

[25]   See *The Word Is Worth a Thousand Pictures*, 378-383.

[26]   John W. Doberstein, "Introduction," Helmut Thielicke, *The Trouble with the Church* (New York: Harper and Row, 1965), viii, referring to a statement by Paul Althaus, emphasis added.

words that you have heard from me, in the faith and love that are in Christ Jesus" (2 Tim. 1:13). Preachers should also emulate the pace and rhythms of good storytelling and poetry in their public reading and preaching of Scripture, as these reflect the pace and patterns of life in God's world.[27]

In conclusion, the best way to inoculate oneself against the dangers and liabilities of the electronic environment is to cultivate relationships and life outside of the electronic network in order to control—rather than be controlled by--the electronic media in a way that maximizes its benefits. This is an essential part of developing a Christian view of the world, mediated as it is by print and pixels. Are you being conformed to this world by failing to be a good steward of the electronic media, and are you being transformed by looking at the media themselves through new eyes?

The apostle John demonstrated that he was a media ecologist long before the first moveable type or pixel were created, when he wrote: "I had much to write to you, but I would rather not write with pen and ink" (3 John 13). Go and do thou likewise!

---

[27]   See my "Preachers: Tell the Story of Redemption!" *Kerux* 15, no. 3 (December 2000): 26-30.

Chapter 8

The Exclusiveness of Christ[1]

John Carrick

If I were to ask you, "Which is the highest mountain in the world?" you would, all of you, I'm sure, without any hesitation respond that it is Mount Everest; and you would, of course, be correct. Mount Everest is part of the great Himalayan range of mountains often referred to as "The Roof of the World." Mount Everest itself, situated on the borders of Tibet and Nepal, rises some 29,028 feet into the air, that is, five and a half miles above the level of the sea. Now, this, you will realize immediately, is not some matter of opinion. It is an established fact that Mount Everest is the highest mountain in the world. Moreover, we live in a world in which there are many such objective facts. It is an objective fact that the Battle of Hastings was fought in 1066; it is an objective fact that Tony Blair is the Prime Minister of Great Britain; it is an objective fact that water boils at 212 degrees Fahrenheit at sea level; and it is an objective fact that Mount Everest is the highest mountain in the world. Thus you never hear people arguing, "Well, there are several highest mountains in the world." You never hear them say, "Well, Mount

[1]   John Carrick D. Min. is Associate Professor of Homiletics in the Greenville Presbyterian Theological Seminary and ordained in the Orthodox Presbyterian Church. This is an edited transcription of a sermon delivered at the Spring Theology Conference of Greenville Presbyterian Theological Seminary on March 13, 2007.

Everest might be the highest mountain in the world for *you*, but not for *me*." There is an objectivity about the height of Mount Everest and about its supremacy as the highest mountain that God has created.

It is very important to note that Christianity deals with objective facts. We are not dealing here with mere ideas, or opinions, or ideals, or aspirations. We are dealing with objective facts precisely because Christianity is an historical religion. Jesus of Nazareth was born under the reign of Caesar Augustus. He suffered under Pontius Pilate. He lived for some thirty-three years upon this earth. Christianity is an historical religion; and because it is an historical religion it deals with objective facts—objective facts which are God-breathed and which are to be received by faith. We see the importance of objective facts in the text that I have chosen this evening from the book of Acts. There we read: "Neither is there salvation in any other: for there is none other name under heaven given among men, whereby we must be saved," (Acts 4:12).[2] These words are spoken by the Apostle Peter in Jerusalem. It is not long after the Day of Pentecost. The Son of God Incarnate has gone to the cross at Jerusalem, has laid down his life for the sins of His people there, has been buried, and has risen again; and after showing himself alive by many infallible proofs, He has ascended to the right hand of God the Father on high. Shortly after His ascension the Spirit of God is poured out, empowering these otherwise weakened and enfeebled apostles.

The context of this text is interesting. It is that of a notable miracle—the healing of a man who had been "lame from his mother's womb." This poor man, who had been crippled for over 40 years, was carried daily by friends, or perhaps by his family, to the Beautiful Gate of the Temple, where they laid him. There he begged his living day after day after day. On this particular occasion this poor man sees Peter and John approaching the Beautiful Gate of the Temple and he asked them for alms. Peter's reply is this: "Silver and gold have I none; but such as I have give I thee: In the name of Jesus Christ of Nazareth rise up and walk," (Acts 3:6). So Peter takes this man by the right hand and raises him up; and this man, who had never ever been able to walk before, goes into the temple with Peter and John, walking and leaping and praising God. Not surprisingly, the people are "filled with wonder and amazement." They knew this man and now they see him for what he is— a new creature physically.

---

[2]   All Scripture citations are from the Authorized Version (KJV).

But the Apostle Peter utilizes this opportunity to preach the gospel. This whole incident isn't merely about a miracle of healing; it is also about the preaching of the gospel of the Lord Jesus Christ. The Jewish authorities, on hearing the preaching of the gospel, are grieved. They are grieved that Peter is preaching Jesus and the resurrection from the dead. Thus, Annas and Caiaphas, the high priests, ask, "By what power, or by what name, have ye done this?" (Acts 4:7) The answer that the Apostle Peter gives is this: "By the name of Jesus Christ of Nazareth. It is in His name, it is through His power that this poor cripple has been raised up." The Apostle Peter, in verse 12, goes on to say this: "Neither is there salvation in any other: for there is none other name under heaven given among men, whereby we must be saved," (Acts 4:12)

We see, then, from this text the absolute exclusiveness of Christ and the absolute exclusiveness of Christianity. My first point, then, is this: *no other religion provides salvation.* This is a fundamental tenet, a fundamental corollary, of the Christian position. Listen again to what the Apostle Peter said. "Neither is there salvation in any other: for there is none other name under heaven given among men, whereby we must be saved." We have here a very important negative truth; and negative truths are very important. It is part of the spirit of the age, tragically, that it dislikes negative truths. The great cry today is: "We must be positive! We must not be negative!" Negations are, therefore, not common in theological circles and they are not popular. But they are very necessary. I want to underline the fact that the Apostle Peter uses a powerful negation here: "Neither is there salvation in any other."

Now, why is this particular negation so important at the present time? Well, it is important for this reason: We live in a multicultural, pluralistic world. There are five great world religions, so-called. There is not only Christianity; there is also Judaism; there is Islam; there is Buddhism; and there is Hinduism. In addition to these there is a plethora of other religions. The 20th century has witnessed the phenomenon of the ecumenical movement—an ecumenical movement which, in some respects, has been a good thing, but which has degenerated increasingly into a movement which is prepared to sacrifice truth on the altar of unity as the churches obsessively come together. It is interesting to note that side by side with this ecumenical movement has grown what is known as the interfaith movement. Thus in the 20th century and in the 21st century you have not only this tendency for *churches* to come together; you have also the tendency for the *world religions* to come together and to merge their differences.

The first World Congress of Faiths was held in 1936. This particular movement has gathered significant momentum in the last 40 years or so. It is an interesting fact that in Westminster Abbey in London every year an interfaith service is held at which all the great world religions, so-called, are represented and at which the Queen of England is often in attendance. The great emphasis in such circles is upon dialogue; it is upon mutual understanding; it is upon esteem; it is upon respect. It is upon the idea that we must learn to tolerate one another. We must not be exclusive; we must not exclude anyone. No one religion rises above any other religion. No, no! All the great world faiths are equally valid and they all, ultimately, lead unto God. That, fundamentally, is their position.

This is known as the *pluralist* position. As the word suggests, this position holds to a plurality of religions. The idea here is that many world religions are saving. All the great world religions are supposedly saving and you will find salvation through them. Therefore, it is not only Christianity that is saving; Judaism is also saving. So, too, is Islam, so, too, Buddhism, so, too, Hinduism. The question as to whether Satanism is saving is unanswered! The question as to whether the Jim Jones cult is saving is, again, left unanswered! But this is the great cry, you see, that all the great world faiths are saving. According to John Hick—perhaps the doyen of the pluralist movement—all these great world faiths are essentially saying the same thing. He sums this up as "salvation-liberation." If you look at all the great world faiths, he says, they are saying the same thing. In other words, it is salvation or liberation from self-centeredness and transformation from that self-centeredness into what he calls reality-centeredness.

To demonstrate how significant the inroads of this pluralist movement are I want to quote Dr. Robert Runcie. Runcie was the Archbishop of Canterbury in the 1980s—the leader of the Anglican Communion. In 1986, on the 50th anniversary of the World Congress of Faiths, this is what he said: "Other faiths than our own are genuine mansions of the Spirit."[3] In 1992, Pope John Paul II, during a visit to the continent of Africa, contended that Christians and Muslims both worshipped the same God.[4] So this is the cry. All the great faiths are

---

[3]   Cited in Hywel R. Jones, *Only One Way: Do You Have to Believe in Christ to be Saved?* (Bromley, Kent: Day One Publications, 1996), 25.

[4]   See Herbert J. Pollitt, *The Inter-Faith Movement: The New Age Enters the Church* (Edinburgh: The Banner of Truth Trust, 1996), 78.

fundamentally the same; they are all saying the same thing; they all lead to God; and it doesn't really matter which one you adopt. You will find salvation and liberation and transformation through any one of them.

Let us examine, then, this idea that all the great faiths are saying the same thing. Why, on the very surface it is preposterous! Are Judaism and Islam saying the same thing? Are Christianity and Islam saying the same thing? Are Christianity and Judaism saying the same thing? And if they *are* saying the same thing, why is it that Judaism and Islam have persistently persecuted Christianity? It is manifestly absurd, it is palpably preposterous to assert that all the great faiths are saying the same thing! You might just as well say that all sports are the same! You might just as well say that American football and cricket are the same, that golf and tennis are the same, that soccer and basketball are the same! Or you might just as well assert that there is no real difference between the Democratic party on the one hand and the Republican party on the other, or between the Socialist party on the one hand and the Conservative party on the other. No self- respecting sportsman, or politician, or religionist, surely, would utter such nonsense if he really considered what they were saying.

Let us look for a moment, then, at the differences between Christianity and Islam. We are being told by the Pope—the Second Vatican Council laid a foundation for this— that these two religions worship essentially the same God. Well, do they? Look at Islam. The Five Pillars of Islam are as follows: Firstly, the acknowledgement of Allah as the one true God and of Mohammed as his prophet; secondly, prayer five times a day; thirdly, the giving of alms; fourthly, fasting in the month of Ramadan; and, fifthly, at least one pilgrimage to Mecca during one's lifetime. It is obvious, surely, that we have here in Islam a religion of works-righteousness. It is a religion of self-salvation. It is a legalistic religion. It is a religion characterized, in my judgment, by the most appalling bondage; and it is in utter contrast to that wonderful religion of grace founded by Jesus Christ of Nazareth some 2000 years ago. What we find in pluralism, then, is the great liberal tendency to collapse and conflate different phenomena into the same phenomenon. There are, in fact, colossal, monumental differences between the world faiths; and it lies upon the very surface that that is so.

How, then, does the pluralist refer to God? Well, John Hick—we will take him as our representative—likes to refer to God as "the Real," "the Ultimate," "the Transcendent," or "the Transcendent Real."[5] He can't decide what gender to use in describing this God, whether to use "he," "she" or "it"! There is this terrible air of unreality about "the Real" that he posits. One is tempted to say that pluralists such as John Hick ought really to erect an altar to the unknown god and entitle it, "the Real." I would remind you that the Bible speaks of "other gods"—"other gods" that are "strange gods," "other gods" that are "false gods," "other gods" that are "no gods," "other gods" that are utter non-entities—the concoctions of men's minds and the imaginations of their hearts. That is what we have, frankly, in pluralism. Pluralists bypass and reject the one true and living God and they invent gods of their own in this ecumenical, inter-faith enterprise.

What, then, does the pluralist do with Christ? Well, this is very interesting. You see, Christ is a great problem for the pluralist. The problem with Christ for the pluralist is this: He pins men down. He puts men on the spot. He demands an answer. He requires a commitment. Jesus Christ is a totalitarian master, a totalitarian Lord. And this is the reason why Jesus Christ is a problem as far as the pluralist is concerned. Now, I say that He is a problem for this reason: in the 1970s John Hick proposed what he called a Copernican Revolution in this whole matter. He said that hitherto Christ has been the great sun or the great center around which Christianity and all the world religions revolve. He said, "We need to do away with that. Let's move Christ aside. Let's have God at the center. Let God be the sun. Let him be the epicenter around which all the great world religions revolve." The reason why he says this, of course, is that some notion of God is, more or less, present in all of these great world faiths. But it comes from the fact that Jesus Christ is a problem to the pluralist. He is an embarrassment to the pluralist. The pluralist wishes to get rid of him. That is precisely what John Hick does. He reduces Christ in classic liberal fashion to "our revered spiritual leader, inspiration, and model."[6] There is this reduction of the divine Christ to simply a great teacher of mankind.

But, you see, the problem of Christ remains precisely because He makes the most monumental claims for Himself. Listen to some of them: "I am the Bread of Life," (Jn 6:48). "I am the Light of the world," (Jn

---

[5]   John Hick, "A Pluralist View," in *Four Views of Salvation in a Pluralistic World,* eds. Dennis Ockham and Timothy Phillips (Grand Rapids: Zondervan, 1996), 47-51.

[6]   Ibid., 59.

8:12; 9:5). "The Son of Man hath power on earth to forgive sins," (Matt. 9:6). "Heaven and earth shall pass away, but my words shall not pass away," (Matt. 24:35). The old adage is this: "Jesus Christ is either God or he is not a good man."[7] You cannot have it both ways. He makes these colossal, monumental claims. He is an embarrassment to the pluralist; He is a problem to the pluralist agenda. That is why they are seeking to brush Him aside. But He cannot be brushed aside precisely because He is Himself God the Son, the Second Person of the Godhead. Listen, again, to what our text says: "Neither is there salvation in any other: for there is none other name under heaven given among men, whereby we must be saved."

But in addition to the problem of the pluralist, there is another problem. It is the problem of what is known as the *inclusivist.* What, exactly, is this position? The pluralist believes there are many, many religions, equally valid, all of them saving. The inclusivist, however, takes a somewhat different stance. He maintains the priority, the primacy, and the preeminence of Christianity; but he does not wish to exclude these other religions such as Judaism and Islam, Buddhism and Hinduism. Indeed, following the Second Vatican Council the inclusivist says this: these other religions are "a preparation for the Gospel"[8]—a preparation for Christ. I want to emphasize here this evening the colossal significance of the Second Vatican Council. It met from 1962 to 1965. It involved, in a sense, an opening up of the windows of Catholicism. A new breath of fresh air came through, supposedly. There is this modernization that has occurred and it has resulted in what some have called a "new Catholicism." In particular, what has resulted is a new attitude towards the world religions. The position of the Council is this: that our attitude, indeed God's attitude, towards the world religions can be likened to a series of concentric circles. At the center is Christ. In the inner circle are the Roman Catholic faithful. In the next circle you have non-Catholic Christians, such as ourselves. In the next circle you have non-Christian religions such as Judaism, Islam, Buddhism and others. And in the outer circle you have, supposedly, atheists. All of these, whether Roman Catholics or Protestants, Jews, Muslims, or even

---

[7]   *Aut Deus, aut non bonus.*

[8]   "Lumen Gentium," in *Vatican Council II: The Basic Sixteen Documents: Constitutions, Decrees, Declarations: A Completely Revised Translation in Inclusive Language,* ed. Austin Flannery, O. P. (Northport, N. Y.: Costello Publishing Company, 1996), 22.

atheists—all of these are somehow related to Jesus Christ. All of them benefit from His saving work, according to the Second Vatican Council. Thus you have the concept of what Karl Rahner, the Roman Catholic scholar, has called the "anonymous Christian."[9] A man can be a Christian anonymously. He can be a Christian without even knowing it. He can be a Christian even though he rejects the Lord Jesus Christ. Even an atheist, supposedly, can be a Christian. This is the position of the Church of Rome, as the Second Vatican Council documents demonstrate.

But how does Roman Catholicism justify this position? It justifies this position largely on the basis of its view of the incarnation. We need to understand that Roman Catholic theology is, essentially, an incarnational theology. It emphasizes the incarnation of Christ. Let me quote from the Second Vatican Council: "By his Incarnation, he, the Son of God, in a certain way *united himself with each man.* "[10] Thus we are being told by the Second Vatican Council in the 1960s that, essentially, the incarnation of Christ saves. The image that illustrates this is as follows. Just as dye, when cast into a pond, will eventually suffuse and permeate the whole, so, too, supposedly the incarnation of Christ in this world has, within time, suffused and permeated the whole. The whole of life is sacralized, the whole of life is divinized, the whole of life is leavened by the coming of the Son of God into the world. That is the official position of the Second Vatican Council in the 1960s. You find exactly the same doctrine in the teaching of Pope John Paul II. Early on in his significant pontificate he said this in an encyclical in 1979: "Man—every man without any exception whatever—has been redeemed by Christ."[11]

These are staggering assertions. We have here the most blatant and astonishing universalism. The Church of Rome used to say that outside of the Church—meaning itself—there is no salvation; now it is saying that there is salvation for all men everywhere, not only for Roman Catholics, but even for the 'separated brethren' such as you and me, also for non Christian religions, also for the atheist. They, too, can find salvation through Christ. Now, this is clearly an abuse of the doctrine of the incarnation of Christ. The incarnation of Christ is a great and a wonderful doctrine. This incursion of the Son of God into time, this

[9]   See David F. Wells, *Revolution in Rome* (London: Tyndale Press, 1973), 80.

[10]   Cited by John Paul II, *Redemptor Hominis* (London: Catholic Truth Society, 1979), 39.

[11]   Ibid., 44.

intrusion of the Second Person of the Godhead into this world—it is a great and a glorious doctrine and we cherish it in a manner that is second to none. But we insist that the incarnation does not save men. The incarnation, in and of itself, is not saving. The incarnation is always unto the atonement. The birth of Christ always looks forward to the death of Christ; Bethlehem always looks forward unto Calvary.

So we have here a bypassing of the doctrine of the cross of Christ. The cross of Christ, William Cunningham insisted in the 19th century, is thrown into the background in Roman Catholic theology. Roman crosses are everywhere in the foreground; yes, but the actual doctrine of "Jesus Christ and him crucified" is thrown into the background. You find exactly the same thing today. The incarnation is supposedly that which saves us. "Jesus Christ and him crucified" has been forgotten and neglected. But listen to what the Word of God says. Indeed, Roman Catholicism ought to listen to the man that it regards as the first Bishop of Rome, because this is what he said some 2000 years ago: "Neither is there salvation in any other: for there is none other name under heaven given among men, whereby we must be saved."

But the problem today is that men are listening to Rome. The impact of the Second Vatican Council has been colossal and you see it in the ministry of a man such as Clark Pinnock. You may well be aware that Clark Pinnock's theological journey has been somewhat strange. He began in Calvinism, moved into Arminianism, and has recently espoused the "openness of God" theology which blasphemously asserts that God does not know what the future is. Clark Pinnock is an inclusivist. He believes in the primacy of Christianity; but he also believes that you can come to Christ via these other religions. This is what he says. "Everyone must eventually pass through Jesus to reach the Father. But there is more than one path for arriving at that place."[12] In other words, he is saying that Christ is essential. He is not formally denying the centrality of Christ. But he is saying you can come to Christ through these other religions. They are, as the Second Vatican Council puts it, "a preparation for the Gospel."

You have here, then, the idea that the Spirit of God is active and present and at work redemptively amongst other religions. The question, however, is this: How is this supposed to occur? Well, there is a real vagueness at this point. Indeed, there is a real difficulty at this point.

---

[12] Clark H. Pinnock, "An Inclusivist View," in *Four Views on Salvation in a Pluralist World* (Grand Rapids: Zondervan, 1996), 119.

Men such as Clark Pinnock have to postulate the idea that this possibly occurs after death through some sort of post mortem encounter. In other words, a man can live as a Muslim, or a Buddhist, or a Hindu, but these things are a preparation for Christ; and, perhaps, after death he will come to Christ, be received by Christ, and be saved by him at that particular point. But the Word of God holds out no hope whatsoever for any kind of post mortem encounter, some kind of second opportunity after death. The Word of God is abundantly clear: "It is appointed unto men once to die, but after this the judgment," (Heb. 9:27). You see, this inclusivist idea is, in the final analysis, simply wishful thinking. Men are prophesying out of their own hearts rather than listening to the Word of God. Their position is, in many ways, reminiscent of the Samaritans in the Old Testament Scriptures—the Samaritans who "feared the Lord and served their own gods after the manner of the nations," (2 Kings 17:33).

Moreover, this idea that the Spirit of God is active and latent and present in all the world religions must also be examined. I would remind you that the Spirit of God is the Spirit of truth. His concern is to take the things of Jesus Christ, to testify to Him, to glorify Him, to convince men of sin and of righteousness and of judgment to come, to bring the sinner to "Jesus Christ and him crucified." It is a blasphemy to say that the Spirit of God is latently present and active in these other religions. The Spirit of God is the Spirit of truth. He honors the truth, and not error. He is not the Spirit of error. He is the one who, in the Word of God, regards such religions as manifestations of darkness and ignorance and delusion, not some sort of "preparation for the Gospel." Listen again, then, to what the Word of God has to say. "Neither is there salvation in any other: for there is none other name under heaven given among men, whereby we must be saved."

But there is, interestingly, another spirit at work today—it is the spirit of the age. I am referring, in particular, to Postmodernism. You may have heard of postmodernism and, perhaps, have wondered what it is. It is a difficult, somewhat complex and elusive concept; nevertheless I will explain briefly what it involves. It is very significant and powerfully present in our society at the present time. Postmodernism arose, essentially, in France in the 1970s. Its roots go back to Friedrich Nietzsche. But it was in the 1970s in France that an intellectual revolt occurred against the Enlightenment. The Enlightenment, of course, had its roots very much in France, as well as in Germany and in Great Britain. There is this revolt that has occurred against the use of reason, against the cult of reason, against an over-emphasis upon reason.

Now, in some respects that is good. In other respects it is bad for this reason: reason is a gift of God. Reason is "the candle of the Lord."[13] Rationality is part of man's being made in the image of God. It is essentially a good thing, provided it is under revelation, provided it is under God himself. The Enlightenment, however, exaggerated reason and divorced it from a revelation-based faith. So there has been this turning away from the whole concept of reason and the emphasis is put, now, upon feelings, upon subjectivism. Postmodernism tends to be very negative, very critical. It tends to be iconoclastic. It tends to promote skepticism. It promotes subjectivism. It promotes relativism so that, for instance, a postmodernist might say, "Well, Jesus Christ might be a Savior for you, but not for me." Or he might say, "Well, Jesus Christ is a Savior for me, but not for you." Or he might say, "Well, Jesus Christ is a Savior if you are a European, but not for an Asian." You see the relativism that is rampant there. That is the spirit of Postmodernism.

Colin E. Gunton, in his 1992 Bampton Lectures, said this: "What is new in Postmodernism is the loss of the commitment to objective truth."[14] Remember, we live in a world characterized by many, many objective truths. But the modern man and the modern mind doesn't like objective truth. It loves subjectivism. We live in an age of feelings. "Well, it's true for you, but not for me. It's true for me, but not for you." So there is this loss of grip upon the concept of objective and absolute truth. The Postmodernist doesn't discover truth as men did in the past; he creates his own truth. Truth is whatever you want it to be. That is the modern idea. Thus Postmodernism reinforces pluralism. It reinforces this idea of relativism. It reinforces the idea that there are many gods, many saviors, and many different paths to redemption.

My good friends, you see, perhaps, the significance of the times in which we live. There is pluralism on the one hand, inclusivism on the other hand, and then postmodernism. All of them are encroaching upon the Church, with many of them being peddled by the Church. These things are undermining this whole idea found in our text of the exclusiveness of the Lord Jesus Christ as the Savior of sinners. It must be evident that there is a massive collision here between what Christianity says and what pluralism says, between what inclusivism says, and what

---

[13]   Proverbs 20:27.
[14]   Colin E. Gunton, *The One, the Three and the Many: God, Creation and the Culture of Modernity: The Bampton Lectures 1992* (Cambridge: Cambridge University Press, 1993), 69.

postmodernism says. I emphasize afresh, therefore, the biblical position. These other religions are, in the final analysis, not some "preparation for the gospel of Christ," but rather manifestations of the blindness and the darkness and the strong delusion to which men are subject as natural men. That is how we should regard them. They are demonstrations of man's ignorance, demonstrations of man's rebellion against God. "And this is the condemnation," says our Lord, "that light is come into the world, and men loved darkness rather than light, because their deeds were evil," (John 3:19). They love the darkness; they hate the light. They love their error; they reject the truth.

I want to emphasize here this evening that there is a fundamental intolerance on the part of Christianity with regard to other religions. It is what I call an *ideological intolerance.* It is not a personal intolerance. We are not personally intolerant of the Jew, or the Muslim, or the Buddhist, or the Hindu. On the contrary, we seek to love them, to come alongside of them, and to win them for the Lord Jesus Christ. There is nothing personal about it; it is an ideological intolerance. We are utterly intolerant of their ideology. We have no hesitation whatsoever in saying that it is wrong on the basis of the Word of God. This is precisely what our text is saying: "Neither is there salvation in any other: for there is none other name under heaven given among men, whereby we must be saved."

But then, my second point is this: *Christianity alone provides salvation.* Listen again to our text. "Neither is there salvation in any other: for there is none other name under heaven given among men, whereby we must be saved." We have here, of course, a very important, positive truth. Yes, it is cast in the negative. It must be cast in the negative. Negatives are essential. But it essentially captures a great positive truth. Negatives imply positives. And that is what you have here: a great positive affirmation of the uniqueness and the exclusiveness of Jesus Christ of Nazareth. This position is taught throughout the New Testament Scriptures. Listen to what the Apostle Paul has to say: "For there is one God, and one mediator between God and men, the man Christ Jesus," (1 Tim. 2:5). The uniqueness, the exclusiveness of Jesus Christ, the God-Man!

Then listen to the God-man himself: "I am the way, the truth, and the life: no man cometh unto the Father, but by me," (John 14:6). Our Lord is making there a most momentous claim. He is taking the name of Jehovah, I am, *ego eimi.* He is taking that name, and through a remarkable allusion to the situation there in the Old Testament at the burning bush, our Lord is taking the very name of Jehovah upon his own lips. There are these overtones of deity in the claim itself: "I am!" Thus it is evident that the New Testament itself insists upon the uniqueness of Jesus Christ, upon the exclusiveness of Jesus Christ; and that this insistence upon the uniqueness and the exclusiveness of Jesus Christ is, in fact, the classic, traditional Protestant position.

But the situation is changing and it is changing rapidly. Voices are being heard insistently and insidiously that Jesus Christ is not the only way. You see, it comes in various forms. The pluralist takes one position; the inclusivist takes another position. There are even evangelicals today who are saying it is not necessary to hear of Jesus Christ in order to be saved. It is an astonishing fact that a survey of the American people taken in November 2001 revealed that 75% of Americans believe that many religions lead to eternal life. Now, given the high percentage of churchgoing in this country, this must mean that a very significant number of those interviewed attend church, perhaps evangelical churches, and yet believe that there are many different ways to reach eternal life.

I want to emphasize, therefore—and I do so on the basis of this text—that this name of Jesus Christ of Nazareth, is given, revealed. Listen again to the Word: "Neither is there salvation in any other: for there is none other name under heaven given among men." It is given by God; there is a givenness about it. This is part of the revelation which God himself has given to us. I want to emphasize, therefore, that Christianity, unlike these other religions, is a revealed religion. "God, who at sundry times and in divers manners spake in time past unto the fathers by the prophets, hath in these last days spoken unto us by his Son," (Heb. 1:1-2). It is a revealed religion! This name has been given to us. But it is also a redemptive religion. Notice the word "salvation" in this text. "Neither is there salvation in any other." It brings salvation; it has a Savior; it has a Redeemer. The sinner is "not redeemed with corruptible things, as silver and gold...; but with the precious blood of Christ, as of a lamb without blemish and without spot," (1 Pet. 1:18-19). Unique, exclusive, towering above all others! It is a revealed religion, a redemptive religion. It is a dogmatic religion. It is an exclusive religion. There is none other name.

I want to insist, therefore, that this exclusiveness in Christianity is rooted and grounded in the uniqueness of Jesus Christ of Nazareth. It is rooted and grounded in the fact that He Himself is utterly and absolutely unique. Let me demonstrate this: Christ's *origin* is unique. He is not from below; He is from above. The Word speaks of his preexistence. "In the beginning was the Word, and the Word was with God, and the Word was God," (John 1:1). The preexistence of Christ! He is from above and he is above all; and though He begins his life as the God-man at Bethlehem that was not the beginning of his existence. He is a heavenly being. He comes out from God, He comes forth from the Father, He comes down from Heaven; He is born in this world. The utter absolute uniqueness of Jesus Christ of Nazareth! His origin is utterly unique.

But so, too, is His *birth.* He was born of a virgin, born of the virgin Mary. The Holy Spirit came upon this young woman. The power of the highest overshadowed her and that holy thing that was born of her was called the Son of God. He was born without the means of man. His mother is Mary. Joseph is not his father. There is this unique birth, this supernatural conception which, again, marks him out as utterly unique.

But then look at His *life.* Christ's life is also unique. "Which of you convinceth me of sin?" (John 8:46), He was able to say. And how they would have loved to have done so! But he flings down the gauntlet to the Jewish leaders, "Which of you convinceth me of sin?" He is without original sin. He is without actual sin. He knew no sin. He did no sin. There is no unrighteousness in him. He lived a perfect, matchless, impeccable life such as has never been lived before and will never be lived again upon the face of the earth. His life is unique.

But so, too, are His *works.* His works are gloriously unique. Think of the miracles, the signs, and the wonders that He performed. Think of the wonderful things that he did. My good friend, show me another man that can turn water into wine. Show me another man that can walk upon the water. Show me another man that can rebuke the wind and the waves and the sea and say, "Peace, be still," and there is "a great calm," (Mark 4:39). Show me another man who can touch the eyes of the blind, restoring the sight, who can give hearing to those who are deaf, who can loosen the string of the tongue of those who are dumb. These works of Christ are glorious works. They mark Him out as utterly and absolutely unique. He shows himself thereby to be the God of nature, the God of all creation, to have the very command of the universe at His fingertips. My good friends, Jesus Christ is the wonder of the ages! He is the great phenomenon of all time! There is none like unto him! Who can be likened to this God-Man who performs such great and wonderful and mighty deeds?

But Christ's *death* is also unique. It was no ordinary death. He died for our sins. He bore our sins in his body on the tree. He is a sacrifice for sins; He is a substitute for sinners. It is an atoning death. He is expiating sin; He is propitiating God. It is a transaction between the Father and the Son. His death is utterly and absolutely unique.

But so, too, is His *resurrection.* He that raised others from the dead—Lazarus, the widow of Nain's son, Jairus' daughter, and probably many others—He himself rose from the dead. "He saw no corruption," (Acts 2:31). There was no decomposition of his body. He lay there in the tomb for three days and three nights. But God raised him up, as Peter himself reminds us in the primary text before us. "I am the resurrection, and the life" (John 11:25), says the Lord Jesus Christ. It was not possible that the One who is the resurrection and the life should be held by death. He showed Himself alive unto his disciples "by many infallible proofs," (Acts 1:3).

My good friends, do you not see something of the glory of this Jesus Christ of Nazareth? Do you not see that He is, in fact, utterly unique? His origin is unique! His birth is unique! His life is unique! His works are unique! His death is unique! His resurrection is unique! He himself is utterly and absolutely unique. There is a glory and a majesty about Jesus Christ of Nazareth which He shares with none other.

There is, as B.B. Warfield once pointed out, a very interesting and important difference between the founders of these other religions and the Founder of Christianity. The difference is this: the founders of other religions such as Buddha, Confucius, and Mohammed, point the way to their god. But Jesus Christ presents Himself *as the way.* He is the way to God. Buddha, Confucius, and Mohammed were the first confessors of the religions that they founded; and you could dispense with them more or less and still have the religion. But you cannot dispense with Jesus Christ. He himself is Christianity. He himself is the way. He is the rock, the foundation upon which the superstructure is build. That's the difference between them and Him.

But this very exclusiveness is an affront to the modern man. He doesn't like it. It is an insult to him. He regards it as narrow, bigoted, dogmatic, intolerant, imperialistic, and chauvinistic. That is his attitude; and he will have none of it. No, no! All the churches must come together. Religious convergence is the order of the day. But more than that, all the faiths must come together. No one religion must stand supreme; no one religion must regard itself as exclusive. We live—and I warn you about this—in a climate of political correctness. The concept of political correctness is moving into the churches. We have now the concept of religious correctness in this sort of area; and the ethic of civility, which must not criticize or say that such and such a thing is wrong, rules the day.

But what saith the Scripture? The Scripture says this. "Neither is there salvation in any other: for there is none other name under heaven given among men, whereby we must be saved." I remind you, again, that the Word of God speaks of "other gods" and prohibits and forbids "other gods." We live, as you well know, in a post-September 11th world. I want to insist upon it in this context that Allah is a false god, that Mohammed is a false prophet, and that Islam is a false religion. I say so on the authority of the Word of God itself that insists upon the uniqueness and the exclusiveness of the Christian faith.

"Ah," says someone, "you mustn't say things like that. If you say things like that you will be a threat to world peace." They might be right. There is an element of truth in it. Islam is on the march. Islam is taking aggressive strides throughout the earth. It may be a threat to world peace. But our business is not to consider that. Our business is to preach the Word, to preach the truth, to preach the uniqueness and the exclusiveness of Jesus Christ and to leave consequences to God himself. The Son of God said this: "Suppose ye that I am come to give peace on earth? I tell you, Nay; but rather division," (Luke 12:51). The Son of God came to bring division, fire, and a sword. He divides families; He divides friends; little wonder if He also divides nations. But we can leave those consequences to God Himself. Our business is to preach the truth and the exclusiveness of His blessed name.

We are living in days when Christ is being marginalized. He is being pushed to the periphery by the pluralists, by the inclusivists, and by the postmodernists. Men today are busy touting other names; and these are the names that they tout: Socrates, Buddha, Confucius, Mohammed, Gandhi, Lenin, Krishna, the Dalai Lama! But it is an insult to the Lord Jesus Christ to range or to rank anyone with Him. These men honor Christ with their lips, but their hearts are far from Him. For if their hearts were with Him, they would insist—as I do tonight—upon His uniqueness, upon His exclusiveness; and they would not be ashamed of the dogmatism of the Christian faith. To rank anyone with Christ, to range any other master or savior with him is ultimately to deny him. It is to betray him.

I remind you that Jesus Christ is a totalitarian master; He is a totalitarian Lord. He demands and expects obedience and submission and commitment unto Him on the part of those that are his followers.

Do you see the importance of this verse? Do you see the importance of this truth? We are living in days when this position is under attack. I want to insist upon it, therefore, that there is no other religion that brings salvation and that Christianity alone brings salvation. Jesus Christ is the only Savior. This verse is, therefore, an excellent litmus test for our position and, indeed, our condition. Test yourself by it. Is this your position? Do you believe here tonight that there is no salvation in any other, that there is none other name given under heaven amongst men whereby we must be saved? Is that your position? Is it your church's position? Is it your denomination's position? Is this the position you espouse? This is the biblical position. The Apostle Peter says so; the Apostle Paul says so; the Lord Jesus Christ says so. The whole of the Word of God insists upon it—this utter, absolute uniqueness of Jesus Christ of Nazareth. Is He your Savior? Is He your Lord? Are you saved by Him here this evening? Do you realize that you are sinner? Do you realize that you have left undone those things that you ought to have done, that you have done those things you ought not to have done, and that, by nature, there is no health within you whatsoever? You are in desperate need of the great Physician, the only Savior of sinners that God has provided. Is this your position? Is this your Savior, and are you clinging to Him?

This truth is so important that it constitutes the mainspring of evangelistic and missionary activity. If you deny this, you might just as well abandon evangelistic activity. You might just as well say, "Well, they'll come to Christ anyway. It might even be worse if we preach Christ to them. They will be more responsible. They will have more light. We will leave them in their darkness." This truth is the mainspring of evangelistic and missionary activity and that is why we must defend it. We defend it precisely because the Church is drifting; it has been drifting for some 40 years or so away from its moorings and its foundation in this respect. You and I must contend earnestly for this faith once delivered unto the saints. It is a precious treasure. We must defend it and guard it; and we must proclaim it.

You see, the Word of God knows nothing of an "unknown Christ." The Word of God knows nothing of a "cosmic Christ." It knows nothing of "the Christ principle." That is what they love to speak of today. What it knows is this: Jesus Christ of Nazareth, the carpenter's son, as was supposed—the man that went about amongst men doing good, healing the sick, raising the dead, teaching the people, uttering things kept hidden from the foundation of the world. This is the One they know; and this is the One we preach, the Christ revealed in the Scriptures. We have to defend it; we have to proclaim it.

The Great Commission requires this proclamation. Listen to what the Savoir said: "Go ye into all the world, and preach the gospel to every creature," (Mark 16:15). "Go ye therefore, and teach all nations, baptizing them in the name of the Father, and of the Son, and of the Holy Ghost," (Matt. 28:19). In order to implement the Great Commission we have to go to every creature; that means to every religion. Yes, we take the gospel to the Jew and the Muslim and the Buddhist and the Hindu and whatever religion men may hold, or none at all. The gospel is to go out and it is to go forth unto all. The Great Commission of Christ requires it.

You see, the great emphasis today is upon dialogue and not upon proclamation. But God is a God of proclamation, not of dialogue. He does not sit down and discuss these things. He announces His word. He gives it categorically: "Neither is there salvation in any other: for there is none other name under heaven given among men, whereby we must be saved."

There are a number of mountains in the great Himalayan range which nearly approach to Mount Everest—K2 and Kangchenjunga, which approach to within approximately 1000 feet of the summit of the Mount Everest. Everest has its rivals. But with Jesus Christ it is not so. With Jesus Christ it is utterly different. He has no rivals. He towers above them all; and He stands, like Mount Everest, unrivalled, unchallenged, and supreme in the midst of a range of tiny, little, insignificant hills. Amen.

www.ingramcontent.com/pod-product-compliance
Lightning Source LLC
Chambersburg PA
CBHW021231090426
42740CB00006B/487